# ALL THE KENNEDYS ARE DEAD

BY

DARREN McCOLLESTER

ISBN-10: 0615658970
EAN-13: 9780615658971

# From the Journal: Chad 2006

## Part I

## For my family

*Cathy, Leslie, Roy, Carlos, Andy, Nicholas, Jake, Lucas, and now Santiago. For Mary and Gordon, who in these pages I call Mom and Dad, but that's their names.*

# Prologue

We walk single file in the sand that leads to nowhere, to the next horizon, for each step forward a half step back. A sandstorm comes and the sky runs in colors from grey to orange.

What are we doing out here?

The insane people are out here.

My mood has been poor all day. Maybe it's because I'm tired of the sand and the pounding sun and the misery. Maybe it's last night's meal; goat intestine soup, I think. Could be the five days of pissing through my ass. It's a tough call.

Closing my eyes I dream of tomorrow, for when the plane comes, for Abeche, where I can sit in an air conditioned room and take a shower and drink the beer UNHCR has in supply, until another plane comes and takes me to N'Djamena, where I can sit at Le Carnivore and hear the blues and watch the singers and whores and oil men, until the next plane comes to take me the fuck out of the country.

There, Izzy says, there are the crazy people.

An old woman sits in a mud hut long ago burned to coal and ash that with each tug of the wind scatters black across the sand. The black cakes the lines of the woman's face, thick on the fingers she touches to trembling lips, arms splayed, palms upward and out, prayer-like, she mutters but it's to no one. Of those who stand among her meager things; bowls, an unmatched pair of shoes, a tin cup, plastic bags weighted with rocks, she takes no notice, and the visitors wander past to a man who lays on a blanket underneath a tree. In his ragged filth the man, like the old lady, mutters, but his eyes are watchful and panicked as if he may get up and run. He doesn't though because he is chained to the tree.

*Hyahhhwwwaaa* comes a piercing scream riding the wind that kicks harder with the approaching storm as a woman on the horizon fends off attackers, delivering crippling blows from a long steel pole she pulls around her body with military precision, finishing each attacker with a spear to the gut. *Hyahhhwwwaaaaaa.*

Damn.

She's good.

What the fuck is she doing?

She does not know.

Looks like she knows.

The chained man wears a torn shalwar kameez, barely covering his emaciated frame; his exposed testicles hang in the dirt.

Hello.

He stares.

Hello.

He stares more.

Why are you chained to this tree?

He grunts.

Why are you here like this?

*Why are you here like this?* It's a question he can't answer. I leave and go to stand beside the old lady. She may be sitting in her own shit and piss but she's quiet and I can't look anymore at the man with the bulging fearful eyes. Military woman on the horizon continues her pole thrusting and some camp kids who have followed us begin throwing rocks at the old lady. I yell at them to stop but they think it's a game and dance around and the woman flays her arms and they keep throwing the rocks. Fuck it. Not my fault. What did that guy say back in N'Djamena? Life here is not life there? Yes it is. Everyone beats on the person just below, so what does it matter if they pelt her with stones until she bleeds? I can't stop them. They'll do it anyway, because they can and it's done to them so they may as well do it to her. Life here is exactly life there.

Military woman yells *sheeeewow arrrryyyyyaaaa* into the coming storm. This sand keeps getting into my mouth and these flies are freaking me out. Man, it's hot. My guts are still twisted. Even from here I can see that guy's cock. The kids throw rocks at the old lady and she chases them now dragging her leg behind her, a black sooted log. We need to hurry and go, so we can leave this all behind where it belongs. This shit hole refugee camp in this shit hole country with the government sanctioned murderers, rebels, militias, pot bellied children, futile NGO's, bad roads, no food, no water, men with guns, boys with guns, that kid with the rotting eye.


*June 27, 2006*
*Jamaica Plain, Massachusetts*

My phone rings at nine-thirty this morning. As usual, Malcolm asks if he woke me. I laugh like always, like he's way wrong instead of only minutes wrong, and slug back coffee to clear the sleep from my head.

He says his travel agent is away until after the fourth and that we'll buy our plane tickets when she returns on the fifth. We'll try to coordinate so that we leave from the same state, or meet up somewhere in Europe for the flight in. It's tricky coordinating the tickets and I hope to defray costs using some of the thirty-five thousand miles I've accrued on my American Airlines credit card. It's taken years to accrue these miles and I've never been able to use them. American Airlines is always more expensive or they don't fly to the destination; Scottsdale and Orlando, yes, and a whole bunch of other places, but where I'm going, not there. Blackout dates for Chad in September? Possible.

Malcolm has a book agent in New York City he's been speaking with. I don't catch it exact but the guy's from a big publishing house and had something to do with the Black Hawk Down book. He read Malcolm's piece from Haiti in the *Virginia Quarterly Review* about his sleepover in Cite Soleil. The guy's interested in a book from Uganda. I ask, why Uganda, and Malcolm says he doesn't know and doesn't care as long as he can get some money up front.

Money. Work has been thin. That what it's called when there isn't any, thin. Three weeks of nothing. News is cyclical and the business changing, maybe even dying, maybe even dead. Today, everyone carries a camera and it's putting the professional camera carriers, like me, out of business. Or I'm just being cynical. Quiet times are the tough ones. It's easy to be busy, to have too much work, but when the calls slow and stop, then the mind begins to run. Do they not like me anymore? Do they think I'm no good, burnt out? Where is that job I had to turn away last month when they asked who I'd recommend because I couldn't do it? Will they use me next time, or will they use that guy? Will I get a job soon or will I never get one again? Who knows? There's not even anyone to call to ask.

Standing on the front porch with the phone to my ear, I watch a woman roll a baby carriage down the street, stopping to adjust the bonnet. Chad is nothing, the wrong patch of sand in the wrong country. It's Darfur they want.

But Darfur is serious money and takes time, and we don't have time or money. And no interest either, at least not from the Chad side. One editor emailed me that he's ambivalent about the refugee angle because they're the ones that are going to survive. Says he figures it will make good pictures though.


*June 28, 2006*
*Studio, Somerville, Massachusetts*

It's pouring rain, more late October than late June. Been raining all spring and summer. As usual the people here are angry, taking it out on their car horns and the barely English speaking coffee servers at Dunkin Donuts.

I said ONE sugar, UNO. Not NONE sugar.

My intention was to come to the studio and get work done, do some research on my upcoming trip, but I'm having computer problems. My Macintosh PowerBook G4 picks up the wireless Internet connection no problem. Usually the PC does as well only today for whatever reason, it won't. I want to call some nerd in Dell-land and demand to know why this computer picks and chooses when it will find a wireless connection, but I know I'll only get a technical answer, and most likely in bare English. Damn the weather. Or they'll tell me I no longer qualify for the Gold Plan warranty that they said was a must when I purchased it. I'd have to go online anyway to get a number to call, so I do nothing and watch it rain for another hour until I pack up my computers and drive back across town to my apartment, where I can pick up the wireless signal on my PC but not on my Mac, because, as it tells me, there was "an error in joining the Airport network linksys." I called a customer service number for Linksys. They told me to call Comcast who told me my router is no longer under warranty but I could talk with an outsourced technical consultant for thirty dollars and that I would have to agree first and give them my credit card number before they would transfer me.

*June 29, 2006*
*Jamaica Plain, Massachusetts*

At my desk, crunching numbers, none of them add up. Leaning back in my chair the right and wrong decisions made since getting into this business run through my mind…and perhaps one of the wrong ones was getting into this business. There was Argentina, when I was going to go there after the crash and do the stories on all the people who were suffering because of the corrupt politicians and the thieving bankers. There was Tegucigalpa and the street kids, being killed simply because they were street kids and in the way. There was Private Jeffries, the soldier I'd known who got killed in Afghanistan, a son's first birthday, a son he never met, the story no one wanted. The stories no one wanted.

## Where Have All The Dead Kids Gone?

It was street kids being killed by police officers, only when we got there we couldn't find any dead kids. We looked. Each morning we went to the city morgue with an outreach worker from Casa Alianza, the organization that monitors the situation, that sent out the monthly report, but it seemed the cops took a few weeks off from the killing, and the morgue only had the usual dead people.

I shouldn't have gone with Malcolm to do the disappearing-street-kids story. After months in Afghanistan

I was tired of shoeless children and garbage pits and poverty and despair, but I went anyway because it was a good story and Honduras is cheap and I was bored at home. I pitched the idea around some before I left but I've never been good at selling and was lucky no one wanted it. My heart wasn't in it. I didn't want to find any dead kids. I spent most of the trip drinking beer at a bar called Tobacco Road, run by a guy named Tom, who'd gone down there a decade earlier to whore and ended up staying. For a few dollars a night we could sit and drink beer and wait for the women to come by selling rare sea turtle eggs and chewing gum and phone cards. For fifteen cents they'd mix the eggs into tomato juice with Worcestershire sauce and spices and everyone would yell *make you strong like bull* and we'd wash it down with beer chasers. By day I looked for dead kids. By night I got drunk on beer and sea turtle egg shots.

## Little Joe's First Birthday

Private Joe Jeffries was with a Psychological Operations Unit attached to a Green Beret Unit. After the Special Forces soldiers would assault a village and interrogate the men, Joe would hand out pamphlets that said sorry for the inconvenience. Then he'd drive his Humvee in circles around the village playing the apology over the loud speaker in Dari and Pashto. In between he spoke nonstop about his wife Betsy. He described her as beautiful. He'd say, *Betsy, my wife, she's beautiful... likes peanut butter and jelly sandwiches.* He spoke about running cars with his dad on dirt tracks and the stars of Oregon at night and, before we'd fall asleep in our bags, he'd talk on about how excited he was to be having a child. He looked forward to one day being able to teach him to race a stock car.

A week of hunting Taliban and al Qaeda, eating MRE's on the hood of the Humvee, sleeping out under the stars in the Afghan plain, I didn't know much more about him. He was our driver, the guy we'd yell at to *stay in the fucking tracks or you're gonna get us killed.* He would laugh and reply that he needed to go the way the terrain dictated, and if it happened then it wouldn't matter to him-it would be us all wounded and fucked up in the back seat. After the embed, the night before flying back to Kabul, Joe marched in a line of Special Forces Soldiers on the tarmac in Kandahar. It's a ceremony for the eight Afghan soldiers working with Special Forces who'd been killed the day before in an IED attack. It was supposed to be our convoy that was to go through that pass in the mountains, but we'd been called off it last minute. The coffins of the dead are carried into the back of a waiting C130, and I see Joe and give him a wave.

A month after returning from Afghanistan an email comes from Kirk Spitzer, a cameraman for CBS, also with us in that Humvee. It read, "Is this our guy?" It's a picture of Joe, KIA in southeast Afghanistan. It said he was from Oregon, that he was twenty-one, that he left behind a six-month pregnant wife named Betsy.

Maybe I go to Oregon to make myself feel better. Or I go for the story, because it's a good one, an important one. It didn't matter. The usual scant interest, lack of salesmanship. It's post Katrina and water stories are trending. In the hotel room on the television there's flooding back east in Keene. The Fox 25 reporter gestures over his shoulder to a loud roar, shouting as if personally frightened; *Beaverbrake Dam could go any minute,* and he hints that if it did it could potentially injure or kill everyone in Keene. Keene, New Hampshire, is my hometown. Beaverbrake Dam has never come close to bursting in all the time I've known of it. It's not even called Beaverbrake Dam, its Beaver Brook, spelled right out plain on the sign the reporter pointed to, even as he misspoke it.

When I pitched little Joe Jeffries turning one-year old to the tired sounding editor at the local paper in Beaverton, he said, thanks but no thanks, we already wrote about that family. He meant the obit when Joe was killed. Eight days watching it rain outside and around the country and on the shoulders of the Gold Star Wife when she goes to Costco for the birthday cake and the yellow flowers to place on the grave of her twenty-one-year old-husband and as she sings happy birthday to Little Joe later in the park.

*June 30, 2006*
*Studio, Somerville, Massachusetts*
*Email from Malcolm*

> d:
> i'e got problems. bosch is getting married 9/16 and i've got another wedding on 10/7. i can't do this trip in october because my deadline is 10/15. leaving in september means i'd miss one of the weddings.
>
> so, i'm back to looking at august. a chad trip from 8/5 to 8/26 costs $2,598 (basically $2,600) from KC to Chad. About $200 more than leaving in September. I'm not trying to bust your bank, but i don't know any other way for me to do it and be at those fucking weddings. They're both good friends so although i toyed with skipping one or the other i know i really can't. i'll call you sunday night and we'll talk.

He wants to change our travel dates so he can make a wedding? Is he kidding? Bosch is a photographer out of Miami who Malcolm traveled with in Afghanistan. They're tight and Malcolm doesn't want to miss it. But blowing off people and significant events is the way it is. When my sister Cathy got married I was photographing cleft palate operations in Venezuela. I didn't go to Scotties wedding because of a last-minute Visa shoot with Tom Brady. Scott was pissed to be stuck with that chicken dinner, but to be fair it was his second wedding. The first time he got married I flew to Florida and rented a convertible and blew my wad on booze and cigars. I gave him a hundred dollar cash wedding gift and break danced on videotape and filmed a teary confession that I loved him like a brother and although I only knew her for a short while I loved her just the same. I wished them my heartfelt best for all their years to come. Which was six. I reminded him of that when I told him about the Brady Visa shoot.

Work's still thin. Tomorrows job fell through. Apparently outgoing Harvard University President Larry Summers will not be doing anything special on his last day in office. No monumental final walk out the front door, no presser on the stoop, nothing. All he'd have to do is wave before stepping into a car and I could get a day rate. And now Malcolm wants to change the travel dates and that changes the ticket prices and I needed the extra time to make money. I tell him to figure it out, that the best ticket prices will be for the dates we've already set, but I know we're back to the drawing board for when we will travel. Defeated, I pack my computers away and pick up a copy of the *Boston Herald*. "If You Could Have Superman Powers What Would They Be?"

I throw the paper in the trash and feel better about going to Chad when I have no money and no interest. At least I'm not doing worthless shit. Although, through good solid reporting and the accurate sourcing of local television news personalities, I find out that most men would want X-ray vision, to see through clothing, and that women prefer flying.

## Random Decisions and Indoor Jobs

The wind cuts sharp, the day blue-gray cold, the people on the street hurry, heads down, faces flushed; late winter in New England. It's cold but I drag my feet, walking Mass Av. towards Harvard Square. I could have taken the train there but I got off at Central so I could have the walk. It's not that I don't like the job, I do, and I keep telling myself that. The Casablanca is a fine place to work, especially after the last job, my first in Boston following the whole U.K. repatriation mess. Mostly so far in life it's been construction jobs, outdoor work that usually involved hitting things or carrying stuff. There was the brief period in Los Angeles where I worked in the Argentinean restaurant. When I went to apply, they asked, you here for the waiter position? I told them, no, dishwasher. It took convincing and I had to compromise but in the end I was hired as a busboy, working in the back with men named Barone, Jose, and Rodrigo. It was a most wonderful time.

From near the dishwasher I'd hawk the tables and see the dirty plates and slip out to snatch them away ghost-like from under the noses of the eaters. Sometimes a question, pimienta fresca por favor? And the diner would hear the cream-colored busboy say, si, seguro, in a positively good and improving Latino accent. After work, out under the overhanging trees, we'd drink beer and speak softly in Spanish late into the night. They'd talk of the homeland and the risks in coming, of the border crossing and the cruel desert, to the three jobs and cash money and

Western Union wires sent back to their families. Smelling of chorizo and sweat, it was agreed, this was indeed the land of opportunity.

But it was in the looks drawn from the patrons and waitresses who wondered why that guy bused the dirty dishes from the tables alongside that other guy who swam a river to get here. One day the owner flew in from Buenos Aires to check in on his investment and saw the white guy working in the back. He shot suspicious looks all day until pulling me aside. He asked, what's your game and I said, no game, I just like working in the back of your restaurant. He didn't believe it and told me that he was restructuring, that I could come back someday as a driver, but for now he was letting me go.

It was my first indoor job and it left a bad taste. But it was late fall in Boston and already cold and the idea of roofing houses in February didn't sound fun. I decided for another indoor job, to get through the winter, to move on when summer came. Through a contact of my sister, I got a job at a burger joint on Boylston Street called the Pour House. This was not my busing tables job. Here I was out in the open, greeting customers at the front door wearing an apron. Welcome to the Pour House, right this way, I will be your server today. It was new. Before I never said things like that. Before, I said, Jesus fucking Christ smashed my fucking finger again, but, will it be just you and the kids today? Never.

The clientele are convention-goers, tourists, and college kids and they are often drunk, cheap, and rude. There are weekly menu tests, and I must know the answers to questions like, what comes on the chicken fingers plate? And if you didn't know it is three sticks of celery and three sticks of carrots and a side of Ranch you received a notice of warning. Spotters were brought in on busy nights to trip up the wait staff asking their own zinger questions.

What makes the nachos grande? Saying, it's real big, was not the right answer.

Spring came and I was late to work. The manager, Paul, called me over and sat me down at the table known as the axe booth. He was serious and sermonic when he told me that I was being let go, those words again. He led up to it with a speech about integrity and grit and the country being built on the backs of hard-working men and how it all applied to this situation and being on time. The place that sold quarter-inch-thick hamburgers named after U.S. states was letting me go for having lost my edge.

I got work mowing lawns in corporate office parks north of the city, and later that summer, pouring concrete for my old high school soccer coach up in Keene. But I was sleeping on my mother's couch in a one-room apartment and, with winter coming, I needed to move someplace warm, or find another indoor job.

• • •

Central Square filters into Harvard Square and I near the Ferranti-Dege camera shop. Looking in the window it's there, still a hundred and fifty dollars. Last nights tips are in my pocket, just enough, but what for? There's nothing in my past to give me reason. Not like I took it in high school. Not like I'd ever had one before. Once my Dad loaned me his Yashica when I hitchhiked Europe on his credit card and I shot one role of film for three months. When he got his camera back he asked how it went and I explained that after a few dozen pictures *the film crank-thingy tightened,* but then it worked fine. That's it. One role of black and white exposed three hundred times, and now I'm thinking of doing this for a living.

There were pictures in the newspaper from Africa recently, pictures of people suffering in black and white. The person who took them went all the way there, to a place no one goes. That person had a reason. Travel had always been a fascination. Pictures and newspapers I'd always liked. It seemed the people who worked at newspapers might lead a good and interesting life. They had been around for over a hundred years and photography even longer, so there was that. It gets me thinking. Gary loans me his instamatic and I carry it with me, snapping pictures of ducks on the Boston Common and a homeless man in a doorway in Harvard Square. The pictures of the ducks seemed pointless, but the pictures of the homeless guy and his dirty beard, creased cardboard sign, blank eyes, that was more like it. That's when I began walking past the window at Ferranti-Dege.

Outside the camera store I tell myself to keep walking, to go to work, to be happy that I'd stumbled onto the Casablanca, especially after my experience at the Pour House. I can work the restaurant nights and go back to college days, get a bachelor of arts degree. I don't know exactly what a bachelor of arts is or what kind of job it got you but I knew a lot of people had them. It wasn't a start from scratch either. I had multiple credits accrued at two different colleges from around the country. A degree would come with some security. And isn't that a goal in life?

The wind bites my face. Looking up Mass Av. towards the Casablanca, I stamp my feet and make my decision, work the night and enroll in the morning at Northeastern. I tell myself, it's silly, you don't know this, it's not you, you don't like people and photography has to do with people. I give the window a last look and begin down the road when that condescending Harvard professor, all 'do you know who I am,' comes to mind. There was nothing I could have done. Nothing I could have said. I was his servant and he made sure of that and for it I'd wanted to smash his face. Instead I curled up in a ball at his feet.

Outside the camera shop torn between the walk to work and the possibility in the window, I try to think of a known photographer, and cannot. The door has bells that jingle when you walk in.

•  •  •

She's at the corner table in the bar, arriving alone, just before five pm. There is a temporary menu before the dinner menu kicks in and I'm early man on until the full crew shows up for the busy night ahead. There's a Middle Eastern plate but she doesn't see it. It's on the other menu, and I tell her I'll see what I can do. At the last job asking the kitchen for anything special or something off menu would earn a stern reprimand, but I was finding this place to be different. The kitchen has no problem with the special request and I bring the hummos, tabouli, and chickpea dish along with a Heineken to her table. She is joined by a sharp dressed academic. He wears a tweed jacket and spectacles that hang on his nose. He has the familiar look of a recognized man; a professor of note, three names and more than that books to his credit; race and equality and inequality are his subjects of expertise. I hand him the temp menu and ask him what he'd like to start with, a drink perhaps. He appears not to have heard and takes no notice of the waiter standing at the table. I clear my throat, something to drink? There is prep work, marrying ketchups and topping off saltshakers, filling the cappuccino machine, work that needs to be done before the others arrive. He's taking his time. He exhales as if bothered. The woman picks at the Middle Eastern plate, waiting, and he leans to her to ask what she's having, the thing in front of her. I say, it's the Middle Eastern plate, not on this menu, but the kitchen did it special. I want him to see the lengths I'll go to please the customer.

He peels the glasses from his face, the anger sure in his eyes. Did I ask you what she was having?

I'm surprised by this reaction, and don't know what to say and so stutter, no.

I didn't did I, he demands, answering his own question, so I remain silent, hoping it fades. It has only begun. Do you know who I am?

And now I know there is a problem.

Here is the dream of roughing up his face, of stuffing his arrogance down his narrow throat in a Hollywood moment where right is clearly seen from wrong, but none of that happens and it only becomes a scenario I play out impotently in my head over the months that follow. Instead I look down at my feet while he glares at me from over his glasses and to his question I reply, a little.

Knowing who he is only *a little* anger's him further and he slides his glasses back up his nose with an index finger. Call Sari, he says, flipping his hand, and I go to get Sari the owner.

It had been good here. The owners, Bob and Sari, treated their personnel with respect and not as a three thirty-five an hour expendable slave like the last place I'd worked across the river. For the first time since landing in Boston I was relatively content. It was a good job that bought me time, the plan to ride it a while and look for something else along the way. It was the first job in a long time that I not only needed, I wanted. And now the tweed suit at table fifteen demands to see the owner of the place I'd just begun working at because I asked him what he'd like for starters.

. . .

Restaurants were less corporate over there, that's what they said. So after the Pour House firing and my summer of concrete, I went to Harvard Square hunting another job. I placed an application at the Border Café. Leaving that afternoon I noticed the manager looking it over. With almost no restaurant experience, I hadn't much chance. It was the fourth place I'd been to and each manager had shrugged. At the Border Café I was asked my reasons for wanting to work there. It was the point in the interview where you were supposed to tell them what they wanted to hear: I would like to work at this establishment because...this place is a great, fajitas are great, the ambiance is great. I need a job, is what I said. He said, thanks we'll be in touch. Heading towards the door, I'd already decided it was back to Los Angeles and the sun and maybe my old job at A1 Builders. I needed to use the bathroom and didn't want to ask the manager, fearing he'd say it was for customers and employees only. On the street there's a sign for a restaurant, inside a man at the bar.

Hey pal.

Hey.

What's up? Help you with something?

There are murals on the wall. The man has a pleasant, casual way. I say, looking for work.

He tells me to fill out an application and I do sitting in one of the wicker basket seats. The place has nice light and

I try to envision myself working there. Bob looks over the application, seeing my lack of experience.

Where was your last job?

New Hampshire. I just moved here for good.

You worked at the Pour House?

Yes.

Why'd you leave?

It was the point again, where you give them what they want…I left because…

I got fired.

Why?

The owners were a bunch of assholes.

He says, you got a tie?

•  •  •

Inside the camera store it's busy, people buzzing around knowing where they're going, what they're doing, speaking a language difficult to understand: Tmax 3200 at 64, overexpose a stop and under develop. You'll get a nice pop.

*What's Tmax and what do they mean by 64 and what's overexpose and under develop? Who's Pop?*

There is excitement. I feel invisible and briefly consider placing an application, but shake my head of the notion. Not this time. I've often been confused of the goal. But this time I know. It's to buy a camera from the camera shop, not to work in the camera shop. Shrugging off the insecurity, I flag down a salesman.

•  •  •

Born in Palestine and raised in Syria, Sari's got a jovial manner and a quick laugh. He's been at the Casablanca since the early '70's, when he walked in off the street straight out of Colby College looking for a job. He began as a busboy. One night a few years later and now working the bar, Sari watches as the owner throws out a drunk. The drunk tells the owner, I'm going home to get my gun, and coming back to kill you. And he did, right there on the front steps. Sari goes from bartender to owner.

He's sitting at his desk in the office behind the hostess stand. I tell him there's a customer asking to see him and that he's mad at me and I don't know why. Sari looks into the bar before entering. Sighing, as if he'd rather not, he nods his head and goes to the table. I go to the coat rack.

The man speaks to Sari and I wonder what he's saying, and I'm about to walk out the door when instead I walk to the table. The woman looks nervous while the man leans back with the nonchalance of someone well within his element. He tells Sari I was rude. I lean to him and cut him off and attempt menace but my voice shakes. I don't know what I said or what I did to you but I was only doing my job and you asked what the lady was having and I told you, that it was a special from the kitchen and not on this menu. I was not rude to you, you're the rude one, and I don't know what your problem is but you don't deserve to be waited on.

And I made an exit for California.

The waiters coming in for the night shift see something is happening and ask what's going on and I tell them and they look and laugh and say come on lets get to work. Sari stops me at the door.

What are you doing?

I tell him I thought he would fire me. He says, fire you? He's in here all the time. He can be an ass. Kevin can take his table.

Kevin's a musician and the worst waiter by far at the Casablanca. He's edgy and once spilled a glass of red wine on a woman wearing white. He asked her if she'd like another. He's standing at the table with his hands on his hips and halfway through whatever the Harvard professor is saying Kevin walks off. I put my coat back on the rack feeling like I'd been in a car accident that should have been worse. I didn't know how long I'd work there, and didn't relish the idea of anyone being able to walk in off the street to order me around, but it was good money, and in the meantime I could look for something else and maybe I could find it before I got the urge to move on again. Or anything close would be good.

• • •

The salesman sweats in the window, balancing on one foot so not to step on any of the equipment. His hair falls into his face when he looks down and he keeps having to brush it back and tuck it behind his ears.

There. That one. Is that the kind where you run the dials yourself?

He's not happy with me for asking these questions. I noticed it right off.

*I think I'd like to buy a camera.*

*You think?*

*I don't know, pretty sure.*

What do you mean by dials? He's doing a wire balancing act between all the camera gear, looking around like he's got better places to be.

I mean I want to do things myself. I borrowed my friend's camera but it did everything for you. I want to run the dials, and I make twisting and turning motions with my hands held to my eyes.

You mean you want a manual camera?

Yes, manual. And I thrill at now knowing I want a manual camera.

This one is manual.

He hands me the camera from his perch in the window. It feels good now that I touch it. It might never be anything more than a hobby, but then again it might too. I could go out the door and take a picture and maybe that picture would be good and I could sell it and if I sold enough maybe I could quit waiting tables. A photographer. A journalist. A Photojournalist. Good title...like it came with an exciting life.

You wanna buy it? It's a single lens reflex good for 2.8's. What do you think?

I had no idea what single lens reflex meant or what 2.8's were. The salesman is looking at me, tapping his foot. I'm not the customer he wants to spend time with. The camera is the cheapest in the window and I sound like I don't know what I want. I'm under pressure, late, and unprepared: fifth grade math, all over again. Uh, huh...

• • •

Ms. Custer entered the classroom and began speaking with Mr. Whitaker who suffered polio as a child and so walked with a cane and a limp. He leaned over her, tall and bony, and she was short and stumpy. He nodded downward and his eyes came up, searching. I'd had been in over my head these last few weeks, unable to answer questions the others seemed to get with ease. So when Ms.

Custer from fourth grade math came in the door, I knew she was there for me.

When they finished talking, she turned and unfurled a finger throwing a bolt straight to my forehead. The others gasped; frightened and thrilled it was not they. The blood rushed to my temples and I thought I might pass out while walking the entire length of the room, past the wide eyes and half-suppressed giggles, to Ms. Custer who waited with an extended arm that she wraps around my shoulders.

She seats me in the front row and no longer was I beside my popular friends. Now my classmates are the ones never picked for the kick soccer team. The boy beside me smelled faint of urine and could not catch a ball of any sort. He's not smart and I'd thrown stuff at him on the playground. Though now, in a humiliating twist, we sit together in math class.

Ms. Custer at the chalkboard spoke over her shoulder. How much is two plus six?

Nine, is yelled.

Wrong, she turned and barked. You, four plus six, how much is it?

But you said two plus six?

Ms. Custer stalked halfway down the aisle to stand above the offender. I said what I wanted to say missy and you do not simply yell out again so help me God or you will pay as the Lord guides me. Now young man, you, she addresses me, what is your name?

This was confusing because she knew who I was, knew who my parents were, because this was a small town, and, just a moment ago had made an excursion to the other room to fetch me.

I asked you your name-don't you seem to know it? Introduce yourself.

I stutter my name.

Are you sure? You don't sound sure. What kind of name is that? The left side of her face twitches.
Just regular, I say, looking down hoping she'll quit.
Well, just regular name, what is it?
Which one?
Which one what?
Which question, the first one or the second one?
Which question what? By what do you address me?
I wanted to run from the room. Like the other questions I didn't know what she wanted for an answer. Did she mean what the kids called her on the playground, behind her back, or to her face, which were, hag, cow, and ma'am.
Missus Custer ma'am?
Mzzzzzzzz Custer.
Mzzz Custer ma'am.
Now which is it?
Mzz Custer, ma'am.
No, how much, the sum total. Her face is a fury and I hesitate while her eyes drill holes through me.
Ten?
And she roared, WRONG, and the kids in the other class hear her bellow through the walls. That is WRONG, and the windows shook. The answer is eight.

• • •

The salesman rings me up and before he's done I learn more about photography. You can't just buy a manual camera and go out and take pictures with it. You also need a lens. So I get a 50mm 2.8, another thing learned, and one roll of twenty-four exposure color film. Outside the store I hold the camera, the one I now own, the one that used to be in the window, the one that could change my life and take me from the customer service industry and menial labor jobs. I tear open the film box, hold it in my hands, stare at it, stare at the camera.

The salesman talks with another customer in that foreign language I know nothing of when I interrupt and this time I know the exact question I need to ask. Hey man, how do you get the film in the camera?

## Our Service Sucks But We're Really Nice

A brilliant idea comes to me during my morning coffee. It's when I get all my great ideas. Using Air-Gorilla I break up the flight from Boston to Paris ($796.00) and Paris to Chad ($888.00). I punch the numbers into the calculator and find it one thousand dollars less than the prices being quoted to me by my travel agent.

I call Malcolm to mention the great news. He seems excited only not really as he's at work and it's only seven his time and he doesn't rely on coffee for good ideas or creative inspriration. Then I call Christine at Stewart International Travel. Christine's been getting me in and out of hot spots for years. I tell her my idea and she works her keyboard. After several minutes, she pauses, and I hear her adding numbers and she gives me a number far larger than what I'm getting online and I continue to navigate Air Gorilla to find it doesn't add in the taxes and fees until the final purchase page, making it the same figure as Christine's. She promises to continue working to find the best price possible and will call me later.

I don't let it get me down. I'm working magic and feel a breakthrough. Good things are happening. I dial the American Airlines help desk to finally see about using those miles. The phone rings and drops off which I don't realize at first. Eventually I do and re-dial and it rings and drops off again but this time I realize quicker. The third time, after a dozen rings, a voice answers and says hello how may I help you, and I say, oh thank god I'm so glad I'd like to find out about using some of my miles on my credit card, I have thirty five thousand and I'm going to Chad through Paris and maybe this can help take the edge off a ticket which is almost three-thousand-dollars-can you believe that, to go to Chad-do you have blackout dates for Chad, ha-just kidding. Hello? And somewhere in there the call, once again, had dropped off, and I find I'm smooth-talking dead air. Anger runs through my caffeinated veins and I forget about magic and good things and savagely dial the phone challenging it not to work one more goddamn time when a woman answers. I give particulars only. Want to use my miles-Africa, can I? She's polite and knowledgeable and quick to inform me that in order to purchase the balance of an international ticket, an extra fifteen thousand miles, I'd have to pay twenty-seven dollars per one thousand miles, and she's working the numbers on her end and I'm doing the same on mine, when suddenly she is not there. True fucking Mobile my ass, and I tear a rotator cuff hurling the phone into the pillow on the couch. It makes a whoop-slap noise and I double over from the pain in my shoulder. When I pick up the phone I use my left hand and the screen shows a blinking SOS. It reads, "SIM card needed." It reads I need a new phone. This fills me with a certain kind of dread. Walk into any cell phone store today and spend the next two years of your life working it off. During the Democratic National Convention in 2004, I was living at a hotel in downtown Boston near the Fleet Center. I lost my phone charger, so in between speeches I jogged to a Radio Shack that had a Verizon customer service desk in Downtown Crossing. The two Radio Shack workers behind the desk looked at my phone, turning it over in their hands as if it were an ancient piece of turd. They held it up to their shiny new ones, two each. They offered to sell me a new phone at an even lower monthly rate with a better service package, all explained in the new two-year agreement. I told them I didn't want a new two-year agreement, just a charger. Six years with Verizon and never having needed customer service and they take back the phone and leave me standing at the counter with a useless Verizon product right where it says Verizon Customer Service.

With this scene playing in my head and pain throbbing through my right arm I drive to Brookline. The perky girl with tatoos on her arms at the T-Mobile shop says, well hello, how are you today, something we can help you with?

I'm fine. My phone is broke.

Well how did that happen?

*By throwing the piece of shit into a pillow.* It got dropped.

I want this over as soon as possible. I feel dirty for even entering the place, like it's a pawnshop or a semen-donation clinic.

And you would like a new one? She says with a smile but what she means is, let me pull your name up on the computer and see who you are so I can see what kind of service to give you. She takes my name and clacks on her computer. Well (she seems to start all her sentences with *Well*) and she adjusts the computer screen and settles squarely on the little stool, you're Daryl?

No.

She looks again at her screen to verify this. Well, we no longer have that particular model, but we do have a new selection. Would you like to look at some?

Like the Radio Shack employees, she stares at me as if I posses the answer to my broken phone problem, easily fixed by purchasing something that comes with a new two-year agreement.

She fingers the phone on her hip, twirling it around on the clip, while a second one vibrates on the desk, reminding her of other things she has to do. I look to see the manager talking with a customer, Motorola's and Nokia's, and he's got two phones clipped to his belt, one on either side, and there's a third employee in the office and he's talking on a new cell phone about cell phones. I become overwhelmed and babble that my desire is to have a phone that works, and doesn't drop calls in places like Boston or New Hampshire. I begin to sweat. She's bored. She chews gum. I tell her Verizon is way better but they shook me down even though I had them six full years and now they're hunting me for an early termination fee with some outfit out of Delaware and I get notices every week demanding pay up or they will resort to other means, and I don't know what other means they mean. She rolls the tongue stud in her mouth.

Well, it's true, she says, Verizon is better, but we're switching tower services and soon we'll have the best. Anyway, we're much nicer. She angles her head. So would you like to look at some new phones? We don't have any of the free ones in stock. I could call other stores; it could take a while, unless you'd like to rent one. Do you have phone insurance?

Later that afternoon Christine calls me back and I answer on my new Nokia. She tells me she's having a hard time coordinating the changeovers in Paris. She throws out times and numbers and they range from scary to oh my God how can they get so much money to go to such a shitty fucking place? When I ask her that, she tells me she'll keep trying.

# Who Goes There Anyway?

*July 6, 2006*
*Jamaica Plain, Massachusetts*
*Email from Dad*

France did not deserve to win that game. That fifi Henry took a dive and the ref gave it to him. My dad would have killed me if I ever took a dive in anything. Bastards. Go Italia!

How much did your tick to Chad finally cost? Who goes there anyway? Besides guys like you and Garcia.

I leave in 10 dayz.

Check in when you can. DAD

He asks a good question. Who does go to Chad? No one really: aid workers and oil workers and journalists, people with odd jobs and made-up reasons. Malcolm goes because he's a writer and I go because I'm a photographer.

This email came today:

Thanks for your message and offer. We are not expanding our free-lance work at this time, but best wishes in getting your work in elsewhere.

Regards,
Roy
The Boston Globe

This email also comes from a youth publication I'm shooting for in the upcoming weeks. In between discussing the shoot, I floated the idea of a story on kids in refugee camps, or kids going to school in refugee camps, or kids scrubbing laundry and looking for firewood in refugee camps; basically something for the 'tween readers of *Scholastic* about children like themselves, only who live in refugee camps. I get this back.

I'll pass around the information about your Chad trip and the upcoming web site to the Classroom Magazine Group. Go ahead with the ideas that you mentioned to me for the shoot—with a vertical opening shot of some kind (interacting with the camera) and whatever else works out. The shoot is in your hands. (3 different looks)
I'm very impressed with your projects. I hope that you enjoy the shoot! Best wishes,
Linda

In her own way Linda is clearer than Roy. Malcolm has a little action going with the *Virginia Quarterly Review* and the *Black Hawk Down* editor. He's going to New York City to meet him on his return from Chad, and just had a clean set of clothes sent to the post office in Manhattan. A friend's picking them up to keep at his office for when Malcolm arrives. He will go straight from the plane to his friend's office and change into the clean clothes, presumably in the bathroom, then go to lunch with the big city editor and try to get a book deal. Now if only we could go to Chad and get into a firefight with a local militia and shoot a few thousand of them dead, then Malcolm would have a sure deal.

He writes to me that he got a second job over the next few weeks until we go, to make extra money, working nights at a homeless shelter.

## Forging Letters and Other Hassles

Today I deal with the general forging of paperwork and documents that need to be sent to the United

Nations High Commissioner for Refugees headquarters in N'Djamena and cc'd to UNHCR Public Affairs Officer Matt Conway in Abeche. UNHCR will expedite the paperwork in Chad, and I'll use a company in Washington, D.C. for the visa and the extra passport pages I need. Without the help of the local UNHCR staff we'd have to wade through this process ourselves and we need the paperwork to be ready when we land so that we can head east to the camps immediately. Malcolm has already sent in his paperwork. He's taking vacation time and personal days from the *Kansas City Star* to freelance for the *Virginia Quarterly Review*. His letter was self written and signed by his uncle on made up *VQR* letterhead.

I find an old Getty letter from my Israel days and re-word it to say that I too will be traveling with the esteemed Mr. Garcia of the *KC Star* freelancing for the *VQR* and I am represented by Getty Images Photo Agency in New York City although I too will be doing this freelance. I spend the afternoon practice writing left-handed so when I sign my letters it won't look like my handwriting, and I sign a woman's name, so I practice writing left-handed like a woman because when I sign the letters with my right hand it feels wrong. Why it takes me the afternoon I don't know, but it does and afterwards I send the paperwork to all the appropriate people and wonder if it's a federal offense.

• • •

My shoot subject didn't show up this morning like we'd planned. She didn't answer her cell phone when I called her four times while standing on the sidewalk in front of the coffee shop in Davis Square, either. I shouldn't be surprised. The story itself is the young woman, troubled, growing up in a tough neighborhood, who, with the help of local organizations was getting out by going off to college somewhere in the south. Unless I hear back from her and the magazine still wants it, I'll only get a kill fee for half of what they were going to pay.

The D1X camera is having problems. Pacing the sidewalk I see it's on when it's supposed to be off. I turn it on and off and it stayed on and then stayed off. I spent twenty minutes obsessing and pulling out the battery, blowing on it, wondering how much it would cost to fix? A camera is like a car; it's expensive, loses value the moment it's driven off the lot, and it's at least three hundred dollars to send it into the shop to get it looked at.

I try her one last time. Janei, hi again, maybe you forgot but we were going to meet today and take some pictures so if you can call me back that would be great. I can meet you wherever, so thanks once again, sorry to bother you, my number is on some of those other messages I left, talk to you soon.

Back home I call around to some doctors offices for information about the shots I need. There's a doctor who has an office on Centre Street near where I live that does infectious diseases and travel medicine. A woman answers the phone and I explain what I'm looking for. She informs me that a yellow fever shot costs seventy-five dollars and I'd have to pay cash up front because health insurance doesn't cover it. I tell her that sounds good and I'll pay cash and that its fine health insurance doesn't cover it because I don't have health insurance anyway. She says it could be weeks, she can't be sure, and is checking her schedule when I thank her for her time. Then I go to Google and begin searching for the clinic in Danvers where I got last-minute shots that time I went to Iraq.

## The Forgotten War

Zabi drives fast and erratic. He dodges children and donkeys and cars and chickens and all the things that run in the streets of Kabul. He only grins when he clips a herd of what look to be water buffalo. I just met Zabi.

Welcome to our war torn country, Muqim shouts from the back seat, pointing to a compound surrounded by razor wire and blast walls. He holds up his thumbs: U.S. Embassy.

With no traffic lights the streets we drive are dark and still the dark unable to hide the decades of war, through roundabouts and checkpoints, past destroyed buildings and men with lingering stares to the Gandamak Lodge. Paula Bronstein is in the Getty room in the back near the garden. She has been in Afghanistan since the war started and soon she heads to Iraq, that one due to kick off any day now. I've been sent here to take over for her.

Paula's covered every international incident and conflict in and around Asia since Timor, the map of exotic travels written into her face. Still, her years of horror witnessing have done little to dampen an enthusiastic spirit. She's sitting at the desk working on the computer, her eyes glowing in its light, an open bottle of red wine on the table, a blanket wrapped around her legs. She leans back and says my name, bracelets jangling along her arms, and tells me the beers are in the fridge. On the bureau are an assortment of ready-to-eat-meals and pills and the remnants of a brick of hash. She says she'll show me around after she's done transmitting and I slide a Xanex down my throat and go looking for the beers.

At the Mustafa Hotel Paula introduces me to some other journalists. There are not many left here anymore. Those that are still here are the ones who couldn't get onto the Iraq war, so what few I meet shake my hand as if we meet at a funeral. I, too, wanted Iraq, but two months earlier I'd been in Mendoza with Viviana and it was hard to negotiate for work, to beg for Iraq, and see her each day, to be reminded of all the promises I was going to break. When I left for Christmas, at the airport in the Andes, I could see in her face, she knew. We said our goodbyes and the see you soons, but we wouldn't be seeing each other any time soon.

Christmas day we spoke and I told her I was looking at ticket prices and asked how my plants were and could she talk to the landlady about getting my old apartment back? She said she would, but I don't think she ever did. Even as I said I was returning, I was still trying to find work in Iraq. But as January wore on, it didn't look good. Then in February, Getty Foreign Bureau Chief Pat Whalen called to ask if I could do six to eight weeks in Afghanistan. I was elated and depressed. Finally I was getting Afghanistan, only I was crushed it wasn't Iraq. He told me six grand a month plus expenses, and I left four days later.

Wais says he's got something to show everyone. Wais is the owner of the Mustafa. He was born in Kabul and raised in New Jersey, so he speaks like a cast member of the Sopranos. From his waistband, underneath his leather jacket, he pulls out a Beretta with a laser sight. He places the red dot on the forehead of the security guard in the next room. The guys sees Wais pointing the pistol at him and tries to duck, tries to wipe the dot off his head with his hand. Wais laughs and keeps the dot placed on the guard's forehead. The others tell a story. Two nights before, during a party at the Mustafa, Wais got mad at some Brits who work at the local DHL shipping company.

There's a DHL sign hanging out front of the hotel, and Wais takes an AK-47 from his security guard, walks outside, and begins shooting up the sign. He rips full bore and the bullets pierce the sign and the walls and inside the guests duck the spray. No one is hurt and the party goes on. It's just another night at the Mustafa.

Paula points to a long-legged guy working on a computer sitting in a broken chair with a space heater touching his feet. That's Dave, with *Knight Ridder*, he's here with Malcolm. Moments later, a bearded man walks through the door. He looks lost, wound up, and bored all at once. He shakes my hand and says his name and nothing more. His eyes give a hint he's been here a while. I tell Dave and Malcolm it's great to meet them and maybe they can show me around, as I'm here throughout whatever happens in Iraq over the next few months. When they see I have nothing better to offer they go on about their business. Paula leaves for the war in Iraq and it's just me, Muqim, and Zabi; driving the streets of Kabul each day in search of stories to tell.

• • •

In the room with all the bullet holes we are watching TV when Wais says, gut sumptin to show yews. Usually this means a new weapon of some kind, only now he opens a cardboard box and pulls out a bathrobe. It's neon lime-green with "Mustafa Hotel, Kabul" written on the back. This delights us and we put them on and take pictures and hoist beers to the power of the green robes. *ET*, the movie, plays in the background and its agreed that Drew Barrymore is hot. Wais shows us a rocket launcher he picked up recently and how it sites easy and just about anyone can use it. People wander by and see us with the rocket launcher and the bathrobes and hear us arguing over who says *ET phone home* best and they leave immediately. That night, with the dogs howling in a hungry-pack chorus, I walk to the Gandamak through the shit-dust streets, past the security guards with the AK's and their own rocket launchers, who wave as I flow by in the glowing green robe. At the Gandamak I nod to the late night diners, diplomats, and aid workers who turn to look. From the fridge I take three Heinekens, sign my name to the slip, say hello to the former Canadian defense minister, and go to my room, where I pop two Xanex and watch *North by Northwest* for the third time since arriving in Kabul.

• • •

Winter in Afghanistan, life is cold. Without the space heater aimed at my feet, I feel I may freeze. We're wrapped in blankets and drunk and its earlier than usual because the day is damp and cold so there is nothing to do but stay inside so there is nothing to do but drink the day away and hope they don't kill Karzai. Dave just bought a new pipe on Chicken Street and we're breaking it in. In between test runs we lean it smoking against a wrought iron monkey Dave also got on Chicken Street. The pipe fits into the crook of the monkey's curled tail perfectly like it was made for it. In between we call out song names to Dave who sits leaning back in his chair, feet on the desk, computer on his lap, scrolling his iTunes. He scoffs when we demand the easy ones. "Knocking on Heavens Door" and "Rock Me Amadeus" elicit sneers.

A few days back Major Bob Hepner called. In the morning I leave on an embed. He tells me it's going to be hot, to be ready for some shit. So when I woke and the clouds hung grey over the Hindu Kush, I decide what better thing to do the day before going off to war than get fucked up. Malcolm and Dave agreed.

*Saddest song ever*, we test Dave because we have not stumped him yet and he's punching the keys on his computer and adjusting the cheap speakers he bought at the PX at Bagram. He calls it his surround sound.

"Billy Don't Be A Hero."

"American Pie."

No, no, that other one...*Goodbye papa its hard to die, with all the birds singing in the sky.*

Dave has every song, and we listen to the words, singing along into the evening, each in our own monkey haze-until its time to go home and eat dinner with the diplomats and aid workers and journalists and foreign do-gooders, and pack my bags for the embed with the 82nd. It's supposed to be warmer in the south and I do hope so because I've been cold ever since I got here.

The next morning I stop at the Mustafa to say goodbye to Dave, who's thinking of leaving. He has a newborn child back home and his wife sends him pictures and video updates each day, but he's losing it. He's jumpy from having been here so long, depressed he's not in Iraq, and his little girl is learning to crawl. We shake hands. I tell him I hope to see him when I return and he pats me on the back. Muqim picks me up out front of the Mustafa and I slap high-fives with the kids who beg there, the ones Malcolm takes care of. They ask me where I'm going and I say Bagram and they help me with my bags to the car, and, seeing my credentials for the base, they say, see you later Zabi, and, Zabi? can you get me name tag for Bagram, so I can go there and work the gate and get all the business from all the soldiers?

• • •

In a building at Bagram Air Base with the word Pressmenistan over the doorway I'm contemplating which MRE to eat, spaghetti or beef stew, when Geraldo Rivera walks in. He snaps his fingers, points, and says Bethlehem right? I nod and go with the spaghetti. He gives me a bear hug and from behind him comes his crew; Craig, his brother and producer; Greg his cameraman; and Greg, his other producer and cameraman. They are carrying two of everything sold at the PX.

Hey man, West Bank. We hid behind that wall during that firefight. I shake hands with one of the Gregs who offers me a two-pound bag of Doritos, and when I turn him down he offers a Commando Field watch, and when I say no to that he shows me a pair of denim jeans, throat lozenges, a case of tuna packets, a Leatherman pocket tool, a Camel Back, a boony hat, socks, and a bag of Starburst. I stuff my mouth full of the candy and we sit around the dust-filled room playing catch up. Where'd you go after Ramallah? That was great wasn't it? Israel's a nice place for a war. Good hotels. Hotels suck here. Venezuela has the best nightlife, nicest women; women suck here.

Seeing them makes me feel better, like I'm not the last guy left in Afghanistan while everyone else is in Iraq. That war hasn't even started but the feel here is this one is already forgotten. Even the soldiers feel it. Talk in the media has nothing to do with Osama Bin Laden or Afghanistan; it's all shock and awe. I ask them how long they'll be here. They say through the embed, then they leave for Iraq.

In Kandahar, Lieutenant Cory Angell and his staff show us to our hooch. We are introduced to the base colonel who's pleased with Geraldo for coming and doing a hangar piece, to remind the American people that his men are still fighting a war down here. We choose bunks, spread out our gear, log onto satellite phones, cruise the Internet, tell stories, and eat junk food. Soldiers hear about Geraldo and come by to sneak peeks into our tent. Tomorrow we will be briefed. We have heard that we "may" be going out on a big mission. No one can be sure, but they wink when they say it. It could be the biggest since Anaconda, wink wink. That last big one that got all shot up? That's the one, they say, wink wink.

A German soldier pokes his head into the tent. In thick accent he says that his wife just loves Geraldo and asks, could he get a picture? Geraldo stands beside him, flashing the peace sign, and after the soldier thanks him he motions for me to come outside the tent. He tells me to follow him and I follow him into the dark and see just barely a sign to my left: Danger - Minefield. It's marked off by white plastic tape strung between the trees. I remind myself to get a red light tomorrow at the PX. We go to the German section of the base and he fidgets with a set of keys at his belt and opens up a lockbox. From it he takes a case of German beer.

It's warm, but tell him it's from us.

I bring back the case of beer, carrying it on my head over the uneven ground, careful not to walk into the minefield or trip and break any of the bottles. When I enter the tent everyone looks up and stares. I am the hero. It's from the big German guy whose wife loves Geraldo, I tell them, and we mock-thank Geraldo for his looks and lure of German women, and our U.S. Army Public Affairs escorts, Major

Hepner and Specialist Marie Schult, watch us crack open beers, say holy shit, and walk outside the tent.

. . .

We stand with our platoons in clusters on the tarmac, waiting for first light. In the darkness the outlines of the Chinooks being worked on by crewmen, readying them for takeoff. Until then I roll into a ball on the ground among the soldiers and shiver. I wear a Gore-Tex jacket and a bullet-proof vest but I still need to stand and walk every few minutes to keep away the cold.

When the light breaks the horizon the men of the 82nd are called together by the base chaplain. The soldiers kneel and look down at the ground as he begins his prayer, eyes closed, hands raised skyward lifting the day. In the morning still, he blesses the men for this dangerous mission in the name of God and all that is good and right amen, fog trailing his words. The soldiers pause in bowed silence, then yell out *hoowah,* and ducking heads against the rotor wash, run bat-out-of-hell into the asses of the waiting Chinooks.

The choppers lift one after the other from the tarmac and whop into the day. Greg and I are on the tail end of the bird. We watch the ground become smaller as we climb higher, then blur by underneath. We had arranged with the captain so we could get on the Chinook last and be first off when we hit the landing zone. When we had requested this the captain looked at us and yelled over the noise of the idling engine, you want first off the bird? Then he yelled over to his lieutenant, hey LT, they want first off, and LT rolled his eyes. Captain shrugged, OK by us you wanna clear the LZ, and when we gave him an enthusiastic thumbs up, he too rolled his eyes.

An hour later and the LZ in site, the helicopter crewman holds up a finger and the soldiers pass the word. Greg and I unhook carabiners fastening us to the floor and disentangle ourselves from the soldiers who lock and load weapons. The back door remains in the half-open position and we go in fast in a combat landing. We slam into the ground and the tail lowers and someone yells Go Go Go just like in the commercials. The rotor wash flings debris mercilessly, and, running from the helicopter and diving onto the ground, I thank Lieutenant Angell for loaning me goggles last minute. Soldiers jump and run from the Chinook and I shoot pictures from one knee as it rises into the air, covering the morning in a disorienting brown haze. All around the valley Chinooks land depositing men, rapidly spitting them from the doors that thud into the ground, lifting back into the air to return to base for more. The soldiers take up a ringed fighting position. The sun rises and I begin to sweat beneath my layered clothing. The soldiers continue to dig in but there are no bullets and no real pictures and so I stand up from my hiding place in the dirt and go looking for Greg. He's filming soldiers pointing their guns at the horizon and he's hungry too so we break out beef nuggets and Pringles and lay back on our packs to eat, taking in the days first warmth. There is a soldier nearby. We offer him a handful of chips that he stuffs into his mouth before sighting his rifle again.

In the bottom of the valley is a village, one of the targets of Operation Valiant Strike, the hunt for Osama Bin Laden, the war against terror, al Qaeda and the Taliban. It's hard to believe that terror lurks within the walls of a mud hut compound built in the middle of nowhere, but like one of the soldiers reminds, as the village is glassed from the hillside above; some of them mother fuckers flew them planes come from places like this.

Many of the soldiers are for killing everyone, but a contingent is sent down the hill to the compound to speak with the village elders who stand waiting, shading their eyes, outside the stone walls. As the contingent approaches they raise hands and pat hearts. Salaam alakum. Alakum salaam.
We're here to search your compound.
Yes, come. Search. We have no weapons. No Taliban here. Would you like tea?

The soldiers descend from the hills and body search the men of the village, going through the compound room by room, poking through piles of clothing and manure and burlap sacks filled with hashish. Some of the village children have come to watch. A goat attempts to eat a backpack. I ask the children if they know where Osama is and they say yes, so I ask them if he is here in this village and they say yes, and I ask them if they want some Skittles and they say yes.

There is movement on the hillside and a soldier yells, runners. An Apache helicopter roars into view in pursuit of a black dot that zigzags underneath. Then we are running. There is a river. The soldiers splash through, holding guns above their heads and I follow and slip in the middle of the knee-deep water and think if my cameras go in then I become a tourist on an adventure holiday. I struggle through the water on my knees, holding my cameras up, like the soldiers do their guns, hearing the Apache giving chase in the canyon nearby. On the other side of the river, it's me and two soldiers when a breathless Afghan man emerges from the hills, stumbling, the Apache just feet over his head, the rotor wash knocking him to the ground, where he struggles to get back up, screaming madly at the thing that chases him. The soldiers point weapons. They yell, on the fucking ground on the fucking ground! The Afghan man falls to his knees and raises his hands to the sky, to the helicopter dancing just feet above his head, shrieking words lost to its roar. The soldiers close in, guns pointed. Stay on the ground. Show me your hands. They tackle him, burying him with their bodies.

The Apache peels off into the hills looking for the second runner while the soldiers flexi-cuff the man who wails, forehead on the ground. Allahu akbar, allahu akbar.

Shut the fuck up.

Allahu Akbar.

Into the canyon, following the sounds of the Apache, coming into and out of view, herking and jerking, it chases a man who wears a dirty shalwar kameez, running for life, trying to hide under rocks, only to find the machine in the sky watches easily from overhead. Breathing hard, alone, the steep craggy terrain brutal. Into sight comes the Apache and the runner passes below in the canyon, a cartoon character, hands up and out, yelling at the lumpy object. He stumbles over bushes and bounces off trees and the soldiers give chase yelling, stop motherfucker motherfucker stop now. Weighted down by flak jackets, helmets, and guns, they are outdistanced easily by the terrified man wearing flip-flops.

When I stumble from the canyon out of breath, the second runner is flexi-cuffed, lying beside the first runner and now they both shower the day with prayers to Allah. The Apache hovers and a thumbs-up is flashed and the pilot peels away and it is quiet once more, save the wails of the two frightened men. They are dragged back to the village and they don't stop the quavering prayers until the interpreter tells them that they will not be killed and to quiet down. With hands still flexi-cuffed behind them the soldiers stand with the elders who explain that these men are men of the village and they were in the hills herding the goats.

Ask them why they ran?

Clumps of dirt drop from their foreheads. Why did you run?

The big machine comes from the sky.

It's a helicopter. Ask them where they were running to?

Where were you running to?

To our village, but then we see the soldiers and become more afraid and the big machine chases us.

Ask them, where the fuck are the goats?

Where the fuck are the goats?

The goats are in the hills.

The flexi-cuffs are cut off and the two men rub their wrists and smile. More tea is served.

My shoes and socks are wet. I nap in the sun in bare feet while they dry hanging on my pack. The hungry goat steals a sock but I chase him down and wrestle it away while the village children laugh. The search is done. The soldiers find no weapons, no bad guys. The elders are thanked for their cooperation and we walk down the valley along a dry wadi to the next target on the list. Some of the soldiers are disappointed they had no chance to kill anything. There is hope for the next village.

The days become a blur of marches, assaults, yelling, and chai tea. Late one afternoon we walk wearily in line when the first reports come over the small transistor radio carried by our interpreter that bombs have begun to drop in Iraq. We stop to listen and word is passed up and down the line. Soldiers think of friends and loved ones and I of colleagues, roaring in Humvees towards Baghdad. Whatever I had been doing that seemed important moments ago was no more. We walk in silence for hours, watching our feet, passing the time. I take no photos when we assault the next village. That night I drop into my bag and fall asleep and do not wake when the mortar team fires the perimeter rounds.

•  •  •

When I return to Kabul Dave is gone. He had melted down, drinking too much, not leaving his room, pissing in empty beer bottles and playing music on his computer daylong. So he went home to his wife and kid. Malcolm doesn't seem to mind because he doesn't seem to like people much anyway. A previous career, years of social work on the streets of San Francisco, have given him a low tolerance for bullshit, and he can be quick to jump on anyone he might think is spewing it. We begin an evening ritual of meeting at the Mustafa after the day's work, to have a beer, and talk about the embed we've requested from Major Hepner and of the stories we've heard about and will do someday when we get out of Afghanistan and Iraq quiets down. Things rage there. It's the number one news story, moving Afghanistan and all else off the front pages. At the Chinese restaurant yesterday, I saw a week-old European Newsweek, the cover photo taken by Joe Raedle, another Getty photographer. For some reason it hurt. Malcolm and I know we are on the wrong story, the old one, the dead one, so each night we meet and drink and talk about how it doesn't matter, that we can still find good stuff here. Neither of us believes it, but we keep saying it.

One night I tell Malcolm of a story I'd read while living in Mendoza, about street kids being killed by policemen in Tegucigalpa, and that I'd contacted an organization called Casa Alianza that put out the report. He said it sounded good and I told him how Central America is cheap, and we vow, after many beers, to go there one day and do the story. Because it matters, we say, like fucking Afghanistan, and we clink beers and laugh at our lies, sitting in the shit room in the wrong country in the wrong war.

Major Hepner calls. We get an embed in Kandahar. He tells us to be at the gate at Bagram at six a.m. the next day. Then we wait two days for the flight to Kandahar, sitting around reading and eating junk food. Each day we call our desks telling them we are in a holding pattern for now, waiting on the big military opportunity here in Afghanistan. Our editors only say fine, that they have to go now because the others will be checking in soon from Iraq.

In Kandahar we spend more days doing nothing. I read and eat three meals a day. I go jogging. I am not a journalist; I am soldier. One day we're told there's a Civil Affairs unit heading out in the morning to check on a school burned to the ground by the Taliban, because they taught girls.

In the morning we gather and meet the unit CO, who is female, and it's not this that's bothersome, it's the fact that she and the rest of the unit seemed so damn happy about taking a trip outside the wire. I try to catch Malcolm's attention, getting into his vehicle, half-glad I don't because if I do, I might not go.

The young soldier driving my vehicle shakes my hand. He too is eager about the trip, as if it's a day picnic in the countryside. He revs the engine and cocks an ear, listening for something he hears best at eight thousand rpm's. When it idles down, he gives explanation to an unasked question, that he carries an AK-47 because it's a local weapon, *helps with assimilation,* and he hoists it up to show me.

Nice. Where'd ya get it?

Confiscated. And he hits nine thousand rpm's and lets the clutch out slow and the truck skips and hops towards the main gate, towards Kandahar.

If we get hit there's an AK on the floor for you and grenades in the glove compartment.

I look down and see a collapsible stock AK-47. In the glove compartment there are six grenades.

What if they shoot the grenades accidentally?

He shrugs. Ever done this before, he yells over the sound of the engine.

*Done this before?*

Valiant Strike, I tell him, and he says, oohh man you were on that? He drops the engine revving and looks me in the eye. What was it like?

*Like?*

I tell him about Geraldo and flying in the helicopters and assaulting the villages. He seems impressed. He says, you've been in a helicopter?

I'm confused so I say, ya I've been in a helicopter, have you, because, you know, you're in the army? He explains he used to be in the army, and hopes to someday be in the Special Forces, but right now he's a reservist.

A reservist?

Ya, he yells over the engine noise, waving his hands around, we're all volunteers in this unit. And the gate opens and we're waved through and I drive straight into the heart of Taliban-land with a bunch of citizen soldiers and glove box full of grenades.

There is one main road through Kandahar and we're stuck in the local traffic, behind a tuk tuk carrying a family of nine, and a donkey cart loaded with figs. In case no one notices the U.S. Army caravan my driver honks the horn and yells out the window, *get that ass out of the way,* and I notice a dozen guys with black turbans and guns who do not smile or wave. We slip around a jingle truck and my driver hammers the gas pedal scattering things in his path.

It's the way you gotta drive in these places, he explains. Guards against attack. And he slams his hand into the horn until the vendors in their stalls stop and stare.

We pick up some Afghan soldiers at the governor's palace, just outside the main gate. They don't look as happy as did the Civil Affairs soldiers, about the long drive and the day ahead. They wear sunglasses and scarves wrapped about their faces, dangling legs over the sides of their Toyota Hi-Luxe, holding guns like they're part of their bodies. As we clear the edge of town I begin to relax when a large Kuchi dog bursts from a mud hut compound and chases alongside the truck, barking furiously. My driver pulls out his 45.

Think I can hit it?

I don't say, but I was figuring no.

Two hours later we arrive at the village with the burned school. There are no smiling faces or children waiting when we get out of the vehicles. The team leader goes off to find the elders. She returns to say that yes, they have a school that had been burned by the Taliban, and we walk with the nervous elders and teachers to a stone building. They tell us that it is very dangerous to teach school in the area, dangerous to even live here, and as they say this they look around and over their shoulders and although they are kind it is apparent they wished we had not come. The teachers have had threats, some have been killed, and being seen chatting with US soldiers by the wrong people would not be good.

They show us inside the building and point to the scorched areas on the walls. The soldiers express shock. Tea is brought and there is much talk as the team leader gives condolences and makes promises she will not keep. Then she tells the elders she has come bearing gifts. We walk back to the vehicles and the soldiers begin to unload boxes from the trucks. Inside the boxes are bags, colored blue, filled with pencils and notebooks and cookies and candy, part of the Hearts and Minds mission the U.S. Army morphed into after the Taliban were declared defeated.

Afghan children come running, the too young to walk carried by those who can. They form a line. The line is long and ragged. The team leader begins with a speech she has memorized. When she is interrupted by a child with face rot, who attempts to say thank you in English, she gets lost, and so has to begin again.

*The children of the United States wish you to have these bags as a token of our caring. We wish you to take these bags and use what is in them to go on in life, to become doctors, lawyers, and teachers, and to someday be able to help your village and your people.*

Her voice echoes off the mud huts and barren hills. The interpreter translates, take this bag of goodies and turn it into a law degree. When she begins handing out the first of the bags, she pauses, dangling one just over a girl's reaching hands. She waits for the photo that no one takes. To one child with no shoes she says, you're welcome. The village elders are thanked for showing their burned school, and on behalf of the U.S. Army, the team leader vows to return and do something about it. Then it's decided to head into town for refreshments.

The town is a few hundred yards long, one street lined with vendor stalls, and in the middle of this town, with the whole of it watching, we stop our small convoy of citizen soldiers. They get out of the vehicles and wave and no one waves back and of this they take no notice. The faces of the Afghan soldiers are tight, unhappy with this gesture of buying local. They leap from their trucks and spread out along the road, walking up and down, guns pointed, looking into stalls and kicking barrels of rice and grain. My driver steps from his vehicle, stretches, yawns, says, be back in a bit. He slings his AK over his shoulder and saunters to the nearest vendor and begins haggling over the price of crackers. I see

Malcolm standing near the door of his truck. He rolls his eyes. The soldiers continue their shopping but the Afghans are on the move, fanning out along the stalls nearest the convoy. One of them kicks a young man kneeling on the ground, yards from two Civil Affairs soldiers buying orange Fanta's. Slowly the young man pulls from under his shalwar kameez a shiny AK-47. The Afghan soldiers point guns at him while our team leader finishes off her transactions. In a nearby stall are half a dozen blue bags, the kind we'd just given away. They are for sale. The only thing left inside is the MRE, minus the candy.

• • •

Zabi, the kids yell. Zabbiiii. Where Malcolm?

Malcolm has a soft spot for dogs and kids. He stole a puppy once from a dogfight in Kabul. Named him Maggot. He was at the dogfight and couldn't stand seeing how they used the pup to rile up the bigger dogs, dangling the yelping thing in the air while the fighting dogs nipped it. So after watching this a few times, Malcolm sees they throw it in a trash can in-between fights, and when no one is looking, he grabs it, puts it in his jacket, and gets it out of there. They came looking too but Malcolm told them to fuck off and smuggled it to Germany. It cost a lot of money, but he did what all journalists do when they blow large sums of cash on things like leather jackets and prostitutes: he expensed it. A few months before Malcolm had begun to help some beggar kids who work the streets outside the Mustafa. He set up a makeshift school in the apothecary next door and his translator Khalid, who we call Bro, teaches them grammar and math each afternoon in between begging in the streets. He assigns them goals with rewards, if they come to school each day he'll buy them lunch, if they come for a month he'll buy them shoes, two months, a pair of pants. They call me Zabi because my driver is named Zabi, plus they can't say my name.

Says the one called Mr. Gigolo, Zabi man, where Malcolm?

Malcolm left over a month ago but whenever I see the kids they always ask and I always point to the sky. They mimic, United States, and I tell them yes, United States.

When he come back, they ask and I say, some day soon Inshallah, and they say ok Zabi, and run into the street to chase down an SUV with tinted windows. I tell Muqim I feel for them because they really liked the attention. He tells me not to worry, they are Afghan, they are used to being forgotten.

## Lying to Mom

Our conversation starts in the usual way. She asks how I'm doing, if she's bothering me, and she won't keep me long. We discuss weather, the night's television lineup, what I'd eaten that day, and eventually she'll get around to asking me about my trip, which by now she will have heard about from my father.

Hi hon, are you cooking dinner?

No.

Are you going to later?

Yes mom.

Whatcha been up to, anything?

The usual.

So you're going to Africa?

Yes. I just put the trip together. Which is the lie because I started putting it together months ago.

And what will you be doing there?

Look around. Go see refugee camps.

In which country?

Chad, I say, and then I spell Chad, and in the background I can hear her Googling the word. She'll go right down the list of websites.

Is this dangerous, The Republic of Chad in Central Africa?

No.

What about the decades of civil war and the strife on the border?

It's all over.

There was a rebel attack recently on the Parliament building in the capitol of N'Djamena.

I know. That's over too.

By the fifth site, my mother knows exactly what I know about where I am going. We've been doing this for years. There was Kosovo in '99. I'd told her then, like I tell her now, it's no big deal, all the problems are over. That was back before sat phones and laptops, so I was out of contact for three weeks. When I went to Israel I told her again all the same lies as before but by then she'd learned how to go to the Internet and search my name. So each morning I'd receive emails asking, who were they throwing those rocks at, and, have you been eating?

The first time I went to Afghanistan my mother got sick. No one in my family told me while I was away because she told them not to. She didn't want me to worry. She followed my pictures online but stopped reading the daily news. Each day she would look for my photos to make sure I was still alive. Her getting sick made me feel guilty for all those times I lounged in the sun in the courtyard of the guesthouse, playing badminton and getting blasted on hashish and Heinekens. If there were any danger, in those moments, it was from passing out and missing the dinner bell and not much else.

Shortly before leaving for Afghanistan the second time, I was watching television and caught a *60 Minutes II* segment. Lara Logan and several other news outlets were riding in an Army Humvee on patrol in southeast Afghanistan when they hit a landmine. Logan's cameraman was rolling at the time. The Humvee flips in the explosion, the shock wave felt through the camera, throwing soldiers and journalists through the air like weightless puppets. Screams of pain and panic are heard and, afterward, the soldiers and media stood around the overturned Humvee, bloody and dazed, including David Rohde of *The New York Times*. A soldier lost the lower part of his leg. It's dramatic footage and the segment goes on to show a rocket propelled grenade attack on a nearby firebase with the camera rattling and shaking and the soldiers running yelling holy shit run and more explosions and more running and more yelling, holy shit run. When the show ends I wait a moment for the phone to ring. I don't know if she regularly watches 60 Minutes, but I know she caught this one. After asking if I was in the middle of dinner, she asked if I would be doing anything in Afghanistan like going outside the wire. I told her no and feigned burning my hand on a pot of boiling water. She told me to put cream on it and when I hung up, for whatever reason, I felt guilt.

Three weeks later I'm at Bagram and about to board a Chinook and fly to a firebase in southeast Afghanistan along the border with Pakistan, just miles from where the *60 Minutes II* crew got hit. I'm on assignment for *The New York Times*. The writer is David Rohde. We're on the tarmac and the soldiers tell us how hot is in the south, lots of attacks, daily mortars: they said it was all on television recently.

How long will you be gone, my mother inquires of my Africa trip.

Not long, a few weeks. I'll email and all that. It's no big deal, lots of people go to Chad. I make a commotion in the background, rattle pots. Sorry, just starting dinner-pasta with apple chicken sausage.

She asks what kind of pasta and where I got the sausage but she wants to know more about Chad and I put that off and answer her food questions only vaguely. When I hang up, I feel more guilt.

## Happy Holidays and 401 k's

Christmas 2004. No one at Getty was interested. I kept telling them I have a possible embed coming through, that I could be in Iraq any day now, but they only said ok let us know. Not that they wouldn't use me if I got there on my own, and that's what they knew. No sense taking on the liability of a freelancer outright when I'd go anyway; so that's what they meant by let us know: let us know when you get there.

Earlier that year I'd photographed the deployment ceremony of the 102nd Field Artillery Unit at a tech college in Marlborough, Massachusetts. It was a sterile affair held in the cafeteria under fluorescent lights attended by young wives, children, mothers and fathers. Speeches were made by overweight retired soldiers of the sacrifices and great things that would be done overseas by these fine men and of the courage needed of those left behind. When it ended there was light applause and a moment of silence with bowed heads and then no one ate much of the simple catered food.

Afterwards, I stood beside Massachusetts National Guard Public Affairs Officer Winfield Danielson. Soldiers hugged their newborns and mothers hugged their sons and some cried and others didn't, and old men stood beside baby-men and, in some cases, it was the other going to war.

Maybe you can get me an embed?

I can start the paperwork.

The following week, Danielson sends me reams of paperwork that I fill out, creating family members and next of kin and signing names as needed. With the holidays coming I didn't want to ask my father outright if he'd prefer to be informed first in the case of my death but I put him down anyway, figuring he'd want to be informed pretty quick, if not exactly first.

To be sure, I float out the idea of The Citizen Soldier Goes To War story to anyone I thought might want it. Getty said maybe. The first ever free elections were coming up in January so I knew if I could get there I could peel from the 102nd and make my way into Baghdad to help out with the coverage. Getty was sending staffers, Joe Raedle and Chris Hondros, and once in Baghdad I could join them and pick up day rates. It was win-win. I'd get the free ride over and day rates and Getty would get another photographer in country without having to pay for travel.

I send all the paperwork to Danielson and the leaves fade from gold to dust and winter settles into New England. It's decided the family will spend the holidays at my sister Leslie's house, just outside New York City. She moved there recently, after fifteen years in Europe. The whole family is going except Dad, who will stay in New Hampshire with his mother. Like summer, the embed paperwork becomes a distant memory. I buy presents for the nephews and prepare for the holidays.

The week before Christmas I receive a phone call. The voice asks for me by full name in clipped Army speak.

Sergeant Diaz from Fort Dix in New Jersey says, time for you to get down here ricky-tick. I'm in the middle of wrapping juggling balls for Jake as Diaz explains the embed came through and it's all a go-go.

The conversation runs through my head. Hi, happy holidays, guess what, great news, I'm going to Iraq with a Guard Unit, just came up, no, won't be able to, no Christmas, don't know where exactly, don't know when either, they didn't say anything about returning. Hey, I got Lucas some Magic Markers.

Diaz is barking logistics when I cut him off and ask if its for sure we're leaving before the holiday, because it's only days away and I don't want to find myself sitting on a base in New Jersey just miles from my family come Christmas. I tell him my sister's baking a ham. He says hold the phone and I hear him speaking to someone in the background. He comes back on, ok, you need to be here on the twenty-seventh, no later; bring the suntan lotion man, you read?

I tell him read and Merry Christmas.

Now, the moment I hang up I have a thousand things to do and none of it involves enjoying the holidays. I want to return the Markers and the juggling balls and no way does Nicholas need those books anymore and Lucas can't read anyway. I'm waiting on several thousand dollars outstanding pay and sweating out bills but as it's the holidays the people who always ask me to re-send my invoices are out of the office for now. But I have a safety net, and I know this; a 401(k) retirement fund I began when I was hired at Community Newspaper Company. I rolled it over when I was hired by Getty. When I went freelance it had over twelve thousand dollars in it, but since going freelance it had not seen a new dime. If my money came in on time, all would be fine, but I couldn't rely on anyone paying me during the holidays, which meant I would have no money for contingencies, things like last minute expenses or excess baggage fees or emergency med-e-vacs. I rummage through my files and find an old Vanguard statement.

Hi, I tell the customer service rep, I'd like to cash out my 401(k).

Oh, she says, sounding concerned, I hope there's no emergency?

No, no emergency.

We do assess a penalty, and then the government will also assess a penalty? She says this like a question, as if it may change my mind.

Do I have to pay those up front?

Can I ask why you'd like to cash this out?

I'm taking a trip.

A trip?

Yes, to Iraq.

Are you in the military?

No. So can I pay those penalties when I come back?

Days later I receive a check from Vanguard in time to pay the bills, throw some money into the bank, and leave for Christmas at Leslie's house where I tell the whole family my neat reasons for having brought along all my camera gear, a sat phone, flak jacket and helmet.

*July 11, 2006*
*Studio, Somerville, Massachusetts*

Yesterday, before I left the studio, I was online looking at general info about Chad and came up with something Malcolm and I had not thought of. Rainy season. From May to early September, give or take a week.

As I read all about it on Lonely Planet dot com I frantically emailed Malcolm with a calm but urgent message. Hey man, did you know about rainy season in Chad? It's about the time we are going so you probably knew and it's no big deal but give me a shout when you can. I expected to get a reply that said he did know about rainy season, and that we'll be fine because the rainfall is only inches a year and we'll be in the dry part. But Malcolm called me moments later. Instead of saying he knew all about it, no worries, he said, shit, hadn't thought of that.

I read to him from the website. Says right here it isn't much, three inches or so, but it can cut the country in half because the rivers run full after a rain. Can three inches do that?

He said he didn't think so and sent off an email to Matt Conway, cc'ing me, so seconds later, while still on the phone with him, I got his email that asked if we had set up our trip to Chad at the wrong time.

He would have said something wouldn't he? I inquire, before hanging up and driving home for my daily bike ride.

In the morning I get an email from Matt Conway. He said he never thought of rainy season, that we should be fine, that we are coming at the end of it, but when it rains, the country does tend to get cut in half by the rivers that run full.

## Wearing the Maillot Jaune

Each afternoon I go to my dirty laundry pile and from it pull a fluorescent yellow bike jersey with black stripes on the arms. I put this on. My mother bought it for me years ago. It's the kind of shirt that can be seen in a blackout or from a mile away. I throw a water bottle into the pouch on the back, put my Ipod mini to shuffle, and head out on my Giant ATX 760 mountain bike for a ten-mile ride.

I bought the bike years ago from Tom for fifty bucks. He told me when he bought it it was top of the line, a lot of money. I hate this bike and treat it poorly. If it were a child they would have taken it away from me years ago for leaving it out in the rain. I actually can't believe it still runs. One day three miles out it blew a tire and instead of walking it home I continued the ride, and because I consider changing a tire menial work for idiots, plus I can't do it, I brought it to the bike shop near my home. The owner's a guy who looks as if he eats granola for fun. He spun the warped tire of my Giant. It creaked, half-turned, and stopped. He lifted an anorexic leg to adjust a leather sandal hanging from a bony foot and looked at me as if I'd beaten a horse.

Ever hear of a thing called oil?

Yep. How much to fix?

He's serious about bikes, like they're relationships that need daily work. He said, you should throw some oil on the chain now and then. You're going to destroy your bike.

Then I won't have to ride it. How much for the tire?

For some years now I have ridden this bike along the same route, with variations thrown in to keep it near interesting. It's a scenic ride through the Arnold Arboretum, starting a long uphill just past the twisted cork trees and out the back side onto Centre Street for the cross over in front of the Faulkner Hospital. Here I stop and press the cross button to get the walk sign, balancing on the pedals with my hand on the pole. The "walk" sign lights and the last few cars, seeing this, speed up and blast through the red light. I know to wait for these last cars because of the times I started to cross upon getting the walk sign and was nearly run over by drivers who yelled out their windows what they thought of someone so stupid as to attempt something like that. The ones who do stop do so begrudgingly, glowering at me from behind their steering wheels for slowing them in the pursuit of their day. Even though I dislike the bike, riding it makes me feel good. I return from this torture a more whole, well-rounded person, balanced, and better prepared to handle life and all that comes with it. It gives me a sense of tranquility. Still, as those last few cars blare their horns and run the red light I want to pull the assholes from their mini-vans and beat them to death or somewhere just near it, or launch my bike into the path of a speeding car and although they would fly out of control and flip their vehicle in a multiple rollover and hopefully be killed, I refrain, because I know I could get in trouble.

From the risky crossing it's on to Allandale Road, facing traffic, slowing to nod gracias to the trabajadoras on their way to the bus stop from their cleaning duties in the upscale housing developments, as they step from the sidewalk and wait for the man in the maillot jaune to pass by. Once I rode with traffic, but on a gloriously sunny day, with a wide open road, I got clipped by a side mirror, and as I struggled with my bike like a jockey on a frightened mount, I got flipped the bird by a woman in fleece who disappeared into a cloud of Subaru Outback dust. That's when I took to dodging Latinas on the sidewalk.

The Allandale stretch ends with a turn into the Walnut Hills Cemetery, where here I sit back and coast and take a long drink of cool water and the hawk flies overhead looking for mice and rabbits and vermin to kill. He floats lazily above while I tear now past the gravestones standing on the pedals to give it some and sing aloud the song in my head, *please allow me to introduce myself*. It doesn't matter what I sing because the headstones don't care and neither does the hawk, but I quiet and slow when I come to the aged visitor standing at a gravesite staring down at their feet. Sometimes they look over their shoulder and I lower my head, rolling past out of sight to stand on the pedals once more-*I'm the man of wealth and taste*.

The hawk is left to his hunting and the elderly to their dead, and I exit across Grove Street onto Bellingham and into the neighborhoods where I nod gracias to the leaf men who trim their motors and turn their blowers as I fly by, to the straightaway of Clyde Street, pure speed, pushing hard down to the end to the circle before the reservoir where I make the turn a yellow blur. On the way back I'll sneak peeks in between the slats where The Country Club hides behind a wooden fence, the finely combed fairways and greens lorded over by blues that never warmed to blacks. Then one day a black man hit a three hundred yard drive and, on a day for the history books, he too danced on the seventeenth with all the white guys. I have a dream of one day playing on this course, but unless I come to know a black guy who can hit a three hundred yard drive, or a white guy who belongs, most likely that will never happen. Instead, I play municipals, and continue to dream. Someday I will be the next Francis Ouimet.

It was 1913 and the United States Open was played at The Country Club in Brookline. He was a caddie, Francis Ouimet, a commoner, and when his chance came to play he needed his own caddy and chose a ten-year old kid named Eddie Lowery. They laughed at him. He won. There is a statue to both these guys on the grounds of the nearby Putterham Meadows Golf Course, original site of The Country Club, another leg of my ride. It was one of my first jobs in the business. My editor, Dave, said go to this golf course and photograph the unveiling of a statue to some guy who won a tournament there eighty years before, and try to make it interesting. I thought it meaningless but with the Ryder Cup being held at The Country Club later that year and some guy named Tiger tearing up the golf world, the story of a common caddie winning a major championship was in. The ceremony was small, attended only by those with some sort of stake in it or attachment to it and comments were made as to how far the world of golf had come. I couldn't have cared less. I considered golf a game, not a sport, played by fat white guys, mostly old.

Years later, golfers walking to the clubhouse at the Putterham Meadows Golf Course often see a grown man, sweating through a fluorescent bike jersey, kneeling at the foot of the statue and praying for some sort of magic that might allow him to break ninety this weekend, and, if not, perhaps just a sign that he's headed in the right direction with his newest swing change.

•  •  •

Today the ride ends and I return home to a phone blinking multiple messages. It's Sandy Ciric. She's been my editor at Getty since before it was Getty, when it was an old-school photo agency on East 26th, Fed-Exing slide sheets to Paris at the end of each news day. She's smart and well-read and, unlike many photo editors today, she's extremely knowledgeable about the history of photojournalism. She sounds hurried, a constant state for people with her job description, asking me to do something quick on the Big Dig. The Big Dig is the costliest federally funded transportation project ever in the United States. They're taking a bunch of Boston's clogged roads and putting them underground. It's twelve years overdue and ten billion or so over budget. Local politicians and union heads hail it as the most innovative construction project since the Pyramids or Disneyland. Whenever another milestone is reached in this great achievement, an event is held and all the politicians show up slapping hands and trying to be nearest the governor when the ribbon is cut.

Yesterday in a stretch of the tunnel renowned for its scope and workmanship, a slab of ceiling peeled back and fell down upon a car driven by Angel Del Valle. He was on his way to the airport with his newlywed bride Milena, to pick up his brother. He crawled from his flattened car and, under the recently installed hi-tech lights, attempted to save Milena who died at the scene, crushed under a twelve-ton section of newly built union tunnel.

The maillot jaune is off, a sweatshirt is on, I grab my gear, and it's out the door driving in the direction of the Big Dig. I'm irritated but I need the pay day and I don't know which irritates me more. This cave-in happened yesterday, and I'd been telling the office about the Big Dig for years but they always shrugged it off as local. Then today it's on all the news sites and now Getty needs it fast, pictures of whatever, anything, because they're behind. Often to Manhattan it only becomes a national news story when it's printed on the front pages of *The New York Times*.

Massachusetts Governor Mitt Romney, a multimillionaire with perfect hair and even teeth, rode into town several years ago a national hero after his running of the Salt Lake City Winter Olympic Games following 9/11. He had houses all over the country and decided he lived in Belmont because Massachusetts at the time had a female governor with newborn twins at home. It was an easy win. The tunnel cave in has him back in town from his sprawling home on the banks of Lake Winnipesaukee. He's calling for the resignation of the Big Dig chief Matt Amorello. Amorello has been chairman of the Massachusetts Turnpike Authority and head of the project for four years. He's incredibly healthy and never takes time off having already accumulated seventy thousand dollars in unused vacation and sick pay. He has a bachelor's degree in history from a college in Worcester, never swung a hammer in his life, but he's the guy who runs the most expensive public works project in the history of the United States. He insists everyone refer to him as Mr. Chairman.

The politicians who regularly go to the ribbon-cuttings are suddenly demanding oversight and accountability, Romney's threatening to sue, and Getty wants this done yesterday. Cynicism sinks in following my cleansing ride as I drive through the industrial lots and dead space of South Boston to the Seaport and the Big Dig tunnel entrance where Del Valle was killed. The sun is setting and I need to hurry before the light disappears. Romney has been attempting to file legislation to use state troopers to hunt down illegal aliens in the streets. Who does he think cleans his dishes when he's done eating at his favorite restaurant or mows the lawn at any one of his fine homes? How will that kind of law be interpreted and who will do the interpretation? Dark skinned man walking down the street, up against the wall. Speaking Spanish? Suspect. Del Valle's husband spoke in Spanish when he did the interviews on TV, when he broke down crying. If Milena is found to be illegal, does it make it any less of a tragedy? No. Less of a payout? Probably. Corporate greed, political compliance, shoddy workmanship: I park the car and begin walking, looking for the photograph that will sum it up.

## Gay Marriage, Again

On the walk up Beacon Hill there can be heard the symphony of chants, prayers, and slogans. You're Gay Go Away, We're Queer and Staying Here ride along on the summer air. For the third time in recent months I'm sent to the statehouse to see if the politicians will vote on the issue of Gay Marriage. Twice before I have come to Beacon Street in front of the statehouse that has been the dividing line between the pro and anti-gay marriage factions, and twice before the politicians of Massachusetts have put off the vote for a better time.

Policeman watch over the scene, directing traffic around the curiosity, and the press around the traffic. Women and clean-shaved men on one side of the street: young mothers and confused men on the other. It is a sea of oddity. Two nuns pray on their knees, fervently kissing crosses. A young boy shouts, you're wrong, standing near a sign stating "God said marriage is between a man and a woman." A glassy-eyed man holds his sign high above his head, "No special rights for sodomites," and on the other side of the street a woman holds a sign that says "Romney's great-grandfather had five wives, I want just one." Because I have done this several times now, I look for the people I've photographed before so I don't have to get their names again. Maybe I'll see some of the men and women I met while doing the story on the pro-life movement, months spent going to Bible meetings and standing in front of healthcare clinics with the sidewalk counselors who fingered their rosaries. During the week they'd hand out literature to the women entering the clinics but on weekends they'd up it and chase the women down the street screaming, don't kill your baby. I needed to meet some women whose lives had been altered by these sidewalk counselors. Ruth knew one and offered to introduce me. We drove to Lynn to meet her. During the drive, Ruth explained how she'd come to meet this woman, handing her a pamphlet outside a clinic in Brookline. Ruth discussed with her alternatives, and the woman agreed to go to a place in Dorchester where she was counseled against having an abortion. She had concerns though, already having two children and living on welfare, but Ruth convinced her that this was not a reason to abort a child.

We arrived at a dilapidated clapboard and walked up three flights of stairs to find the young woman not at home. We stood around among the children's toys and tossed a ball to a little boy in diapers who wobbled after it and waited with the cousins and the neighbors watching television on the big screen, nestled between two speakers, under the VCR, below the stereo, and above the video game console. When the woman arrived she looked tired and not happy to see Ruth or me.

The foes of gay marriage yell at the proponents, back and forth across the street, and in the crowd a man shoulders a cross with a limp Jesus nailed to it. He's holding it upward and praying towards the statehouse with his head on his chest. He sways backward and forward as if he may fall to the ground. His chest vibrates like a purring cat. An older woman emerges from the crowd to touch the feet of Jesus and leans and mutters falling into rhythm alongside the purring man. She breaks from her prayers to draw the sign of the cross over her chest.

Who do you work for? She is looking at me from behind fogged glasses.

She appears harmless but these questions are tricky and the answer might depend. At a World Economic Forum meeting in New York City I was asked by a young man with three nose rings and pants made of hemp, shouting, "Death to corporate America," who do you work for? With police officers nearby I told the young man in a firm voice, Getty. In Afghanistan surrounded by angry men wearing eyeliner and holding Korans, chanting, "Death to America," I was asked again, who do you work for? With no police officers nearby I told them, no hablo inglese, and got the hell out of there. Now this woman with the God Save Marriage T-shirt demands to know who employs me. She's old and there are cops around and I've got time to kill so I say I work for myself but I freelance for whoever, like Getty, but sometimes I work for their other departments, like assignments, or editorial, or entertainment-but this is for the news wire 'cause its news worthy, and sometimes people just call each other and ask who do you use in Boston, and then sometimes people just call me directly.

She says, *who* do you work for?

I look over her head and wait for the cross-carrying guy to stop his prayers so I can get his name. Not my problem if she doesn't understand the business. She stares at me from under my chin, repeating her question. Her demand to know who I'm working for irritates me because my answer irritates me. When it's spoken out loud or explained in any way, it doesn't sound like anything. I tell her again, Getty Images.

She's suspicious. She says, who are they and where will these photographs be published? She touches my chest with shaky fingers. Please, just, I want you to show us in the right light. The media makes us out so poorly. I beg of you to please show the people who we really are, and she reaches for the praying man's cross and pulls it down to her lips now dripping with religious spittle, and they quiver when she kisses it, leaving wet marks on the feet of Jesus. She raises her hands and face to the sky and statehouse. We are human too, and He died for all our sins.

*Praise the Lord.*

At six o'clock, shortly after the last major news cycle of the evening, the politicians of Massachusetts vote once again to put off the vote, once again, on gay marriage-until just after the upcoming November general elections.

## The Family Picnic

Spent the weekend in Rye Beach in New Hampshire at the Drake House where my father lives in a third-floor apartment that overlooks the Isle of Shoals. Each year we have a family barbeque, generally in the fall, but this year it comes in summer. Leslie is in from Europe with her husband Carlos and sons Nick and Jake. Cathy and Andy live in nearby Stratham with their son Lucas and my mother and stepfather Roy live just down the road from my father and they are all there. Sometimes my grandmother comes from Keene, and my Aunt Evelyn from Spofford, and we invite all the friends we have, although each year fewer seem to come. It occurs to none of us that we would never go to another family's reunion, but we know there's no getting out of our own, mostly because all the good excuses have been made up by our friends not coming. Sickness; last-minute work; car got stolen; kids have soccer, flu, the measles; they are all taken or have been used in the past, so we congregate poolside each year at Dad's house, across the street from the Atlantic, on an acre of thick, green grass where the nephews can run like dogs and chase every kind of ball we have, which is every kind of ball there is. Between that they take numerous breaks to eat and drink and to jump in the pool. Then they will find me and ask nonstop questions of which game I'd like to play next, even though I didn't play the last.

Uncle D, do you want to play soccer?

I have learned they will not take no I'm drinking beer as a proper excuse. They know I like balls myself and I may have mentioned my 1983 New Hampshire state soccer title won in my junior year and how we lost my senior year after a thirty-two game win streak in a double overtime shoot out to that shit town Nashua. So, I feed seven-year-old Nicholas crosses and he rockets balls at four-year-old Jake in goal who stops them with younger-brother intensity and various body parts, including head and face, until I call for a timeout. They'll agree to the timeout and, after a dip in the pool, they'll find me hiding behind the grill.

Uncle D, wanna play soccer some more.

Not right now.

Tag?

No.

Baseball?

How bout just a little break?

Ok, then baseball?

Maybe then baseball.

Ok, right after your little break maybe then baseball.

Right after.

And they never forget.

On Saturday night, Carlos and Andy mentioned to their wives that they thought it would be a good idea for the three of us to head into Portsmouth to have a few beers at the Brewery. After years of being married to my sisters my brothers-in-law have learned they can preface anything they'd like to do with, *your brother and I would like to*-and they can fill in the blank. My sisters will always agree, urging them to spend time with their brother-in-law as if it were their idea. It is a good trick and has worked many times in the past, but recently I have begun to see that my nephews have caught on when three-year-old Lucas, after being put to bed twice, came down from upstairs and told his mother, I wanna watch TV with Uncle D, and his mother said, ohhh you wanna spend time with your Uncle? And before I knew it we are not watching the Red Sox anymore; we are watching *Harold and the Purple Crayon.*

The Portsmouth Brewery hops, full of college students. We get two stools and standing room at the bar corner. We hoist drinks and say salud to another year, and Carlos excuses himself to step outside to smoke with strangers and Andy nods off. He's a four a.m. riser, and this is also something I've noticed about my brothers-in-law, that with no wife or child nearby, they will take that as an opportunity to nap. I have watched them look around, see no family, and nod off leaning against a wall.

I nurse my beer alone, in thoughts of my upcoming trip, and Andy snorts and wakes and the bartender gives us a free Red Bull. Carlos returns, smelling of cigars. They both look rested and content, and I feel good in being able to help them enjoy a tranquil night out, and on the walk from the bar to the car, we stop to buy soft shell lobsters.

The moon is full, and under it we sit on the patio outside Dad's apartment. The ocean pounds in the night, the moonlight bouncing blue and gold off the surface of the pool. The screams of the lobsters thrown alive on the grill have echoed away and we sit sucking at the spindly little legs. Before we are off to bed, Andy leans to me and asks quietly if I wouldn't mention to Cathy that he slept a little at the bar and, after Andy leaves, Carlos leans to me and says, please don't tell your sister I smoked cigars. I tell them both the same thing; stays with me and you, brother.

Early the next morning the sun rises over the Isle of Shoals and wakes me sleeping on the couch, bathing me in a terrific light. It's beautiful, serene, and the bright of it crushes my skull, the heat already unbearable, and I think I may puke up that lobster I ate at two a.m. Rolling over in the twisted blankets and about to fall back asleep, my nephews stumble into the room.

Hi Uncle D. Wanna play soccer?

Dad leaves for Turkey over the weekend. He times his yearly travel for two days after family get togethers begin. No one takes it personally; mostly we are jealous we didn't think of it ourselves. Leslie doesn't mind either because when he leaves she takes over his apartment at the Drake House. Due notice is given each year to the other Drake House tenants of the upcoming picnic. Now, when they see a member of Leslie's family, they will say, where is your father off to? Or when my father informs them that he's going away they will ask, when does Leslie arrive? This year, like the friends we invite that don't come, I notice less Drake House tenants at the pool than last year. I wonder if perhaps Dad might bump into some of them in Istanbul.

My nephews see my father leaving, bag over his shoulder, smile on his face, energy in his step. Over the years they have asked many questions about my travels and I've pointed out to them on a globe some of the places I have been. Because of this, and because they have a natural ability to terrorize their mothers, they will say, Mom, after I go to Kandahar, I'd like to visit Managua.

Now I leave, exhausted from my early morning wake up and the scoring of the goals all before breakfast. From the car I say to my nephews, standing in the driveway, that I will see them again soon and will show them pictures from my trip when I do. They wave and run off to play a game involving balls and hitting, except for Nicholas, my eldest nephew, who steps closer to the car. He asks, Uncle D why are you going to Chad? And I find I have no good answer.

## First Descents

The single engine aircraft jostles violently in the turbulence and I lean my head on my forearm and gag back vomit. Every person on the plane smokes, and I hold on desperately as we descend to the ground. We will be landing soon, Inshallah, says the man beside me between exhales on a no-filter. I pray Inshallah makes it fast because I need to throw up.

With a bump onto the ground, the flight steward takes the cigarette from between her teeth and welcomes us to Skopje International Airport. I step outside into the sun and walk down the rollaway stairs to the tarmac, sucking in the fresh air, thanking God nothing moves anymore beneath my feet. Bending at the waist I breathe deeply through my nose and rummage in my pack for a Pepto-Bismol tablet. Rubbing the pink tablet over my tongue and gums, a dozen soldiers stare at me. They point. I try to straighten. My head swims and stomach turns and I drop to my knees and dry heave near the plane tires until water streams from my eyes.

The customs man wears a funny hat and ignores my tears. He demands my passport. Not taking his eyes from me, he stamps the first page he opens to. I look at the new stamp, the first good one, the first real one. Outside, a slew of taxi drivers yell for my business and in the fumes of broke old cars my nausea returns. A young man says over the yelling and shoving, come with me, I will take you, and I follow him through the crowd that pulls at me. I need a hotel for the night, just one night, I tell him, and after a bit with some hand motions and a drawing on the dashboard, he smiles. Otel otel. He knows a guy and begins driving. I sink back into the seat, happy for no more smoke, feeling the buzzing din in my head begin to lessen. The driver picks up a pack of Marlboro knock-offs, shakes one out, lights it, inhales deep and exhales. He offers me one.

At the hotel after check in I negotiate with the driver for a ride to the border in the morning. He will come early and take me. He is happy with already having a job lined up for tomorrow and I give him extra to make sure. He stands in the doorway holding up his hands, one with five fingers, the other with two, and points at his toes. Yes, seven a.m., here.

The evening air is warm and I need to eat something to try and settle my stomach. I find a Chinese restaurant not far from the hotel. The waiter takes my order and places it with the kitchen and it's just me and him in this outdoor Chinese café. Where are you from, he asks, and why I don't know, because he appears to be friendly, I find myself wanting to lie. United States, I tell him the truth. He says the United States is nice. You come here for Kosovo? I tell him I leave in the morning. He whistles through his teeth. Bad things happen there. Someday that war comes here.

I eat the fried rice and pay the bill and say goodbye to the waiter, walking the street as the sun sets, my stomach feeling better by the step. Soon I'll fall asleep and in the morning it's to the border and who knew what.

At a four-way intersection Gypsy kids beg from the passing cars. They wear tattered, ill-fitting clothes, grimed by the exhaust of the vehicles whose windows they tap on during the red lights. The souls of their feet are black and thick from a shoeless lifetime, their teeth colored and chipped, hair matted. A woman carries a newborn wrapped in a filthy blanket in-between the lines of traffic, holding him up to the windows, gesturing to the child's mouth. The children see me and run to me holding up their hands. It's a game I think and slap open palms and they slap back but continue holding out their hands, rubbing greasy fingers together. I rummage in my pockets for the left-over money from the Chinese food, local money. I give it to the shoeless children. They look down, frown, and hurl the coins into the street. They spit at me what sound like unkind words and return to their begging in the lines of the passing traffic.

•  •  •

The border nears. Trucks carrying supplies line the road, waiting for their turn to cross, disappearing into the distance. A refugee camp has sprouted from the ground, a sprawl of tents and hanging laundry and wood smoke drifting gray into the day. The driver points and speaks but I understand little and say nothing. He stops a quarter mile from the checkpoint. He will go no further. He apologizes. I pull bags from the trunk. He asks when I return, that he will be there waiting for me when I do. Looking past the trucks and roadside hawkers to the border, I shake my head. He shrugs, grasps my hand, gets into his cab, and drives back down the road to Skopje.

•  •  •

The year before I get hired to work at Community Newspaper Company, shooting for the city weeklies. After leaving the Casablanca I'd been freelancing at CNC for a year when a job comes up in the Needham office covering Boston and metro-west. It was between me and another guy named Rey Banogon. Photo editor Dave Del Poio protects his photographers the way a trainer does his fighters. Many a newly hired just starting out writer has attempted to drop a photo assignment onto his desk only to have him pick it up, read it, casually hand it back, and say, not gonna happen. When asked why he'd be clear on the explanation; because I'm not going to waste my photographers time with this bullshit.

He calls me into the office for an interview and I feel good about my chances. I'd just finished an essay on homeless alcoholics and was working another one on a politician named Dapper. Dave knew I was running hot, that I was hungry, that I needed a job. We sat down in the conference room.

I'm giving the job to Rey.

What? Why? That figures. Cause he's Asian right?

No. He's been here longer. And he's good.

It was true. Rey had been there longer and he was good. It's just I wanted a better reason. Rey getting picked meant me having to continue freelancing for ten dollars an assignment versus eight dollars an hour. It had been a tough year since quitting the Casablanca and I was barely making ends meet. Even with the occasional fifteen-dollar sports assignment I was finding it difficult. So Rey getting hired over me hurt. I wanted the financial security of that eight dollars times forty each week. On the way out of the conference room Dave tells me that the next job to open up will be mine. Rey's job was the first to open in the photography department at CNC in years. There were dozens of applicants. I tell Dave his words mean nothing and I'm going to stick his stupid decision up his ass either way.

I double my assignment load, take the night and weekend ones, shooting two-dozen jobs seven days a week. Rey becomes my roommate. Another position opens and I apologize to Dave for anything he thought he might have heard in the last interview. I become a thirty-two year old professional photojournalist with minimal experience making seventeen thousand five hundred dollars a year.

The job comes with a 401(k) plan, so I can retire in comfort later in life.

• • •

The border guard shifts the AK-47 onto his shoulder and pokes through my bags, turning over the gear and holding up a Power Bar. He waves a hand past the razor wire and tanks. I gather my things, spread out around the table, and put them back into my bags. For this trip I'd taken two weeks of vacation time, three sick days, two personal days, and a mental health day. My bank account is empty and most of the seventeen hundred dollars is stuffed into a money pouch and both shoes.

Men idle by the edge of the road loitering near cars parked in the shade, smoking cigarettes to the nub, watching the other man from the outside world walk up from the checkpoint.

Where you go?

The capitol.

One hundred.

Too much.

Ninety?

No.

They throw down cigarettes in disgust and wave hands at the cars, to the smoking piles of garbage, to the tanks and the soldiers, and they go back to sitting on the vehicles that have no gas anyway. One young man takes the elbow of the foreigner. I have car, come, pay what you like, and this sounds good so the man throws his bags into the backseat and they begin on the road to Pristina.

The road winds through a mess of scarred countryside with burned homes and drifting smoke. Garbage and dead animals litter the roadside, bloated oozing lumps that split open in the heat. The passing cars momentarily scatter the dogs and birds that eat the red goo. The driver points to a village in the distance that used to be. He stops the car and leads down a path. His hands are upon his chest. Mounds covered with red plastic sheeting and fake flowers extend to the horizon, where they touch the ruined buildings, bouncing back to where we stand. The driver looks at the mounds, speaking from under his breath. He kneels and fingers one of the fake flowers. The ribbon marker says the mound was eighteen, male, had died two months before. He pinches his eyes, muttering, and we return to the car and continue down the scarred road.

In the lobby of the Grand Hotel a young man sits in a torn chair chain-smoking cigarettes. I feel his eyes upon my back as I check in. When I turn for the stairs he is there.

Do you need driver or translator? He speaks good English, or good enough, and I do need a driver/translator. I tell him in the morning I want to take a trip to Gjilane to find a woman from the International Rescue Committee. Before leaving I'd read of this woman who attended Tufts University and now works for the IRC in Gjilane. Tufts is in Somerville, one of the towns I cover, so if I can find her I can do a local story for the *Somerville Journal*. It gives me a byline from a foreign country and although Dave had told me he couldn't pay me, if I do find her and do a story, he might be able to give me back some of the vacation days I've taken.

The young man knows Gjilane, knows where IRC is. His name is Junus and he has worked for many journalists since the war began. He will take me. That night the echoes of the war-maddened dogs running loose in the capitol keep me awake.

Junus arrives early the next morning. He drives us across town to a cinderblock building pocked from heavy shelling. We go up the stairs through the dank hallways where water drips down the walls and people used to live but now the apartments are mostly empty. He says over his shoulder that perhaps I would like to take tea with his family. His parents greet us at the door. A young woman comes from a back room with a newborn in her arms. Junus pats the child's head, and a pot of water is placed on a hotplate. We drink the tea in the main room with the clean couch, brushed each day by the mother of Junus, who continues to strive for normalcy, while little pieces of plaster drop from the ceiling onto our shoulders. They speak of the months of bombing and of surviving the war, as if they have; Junus sneaking out of the house to search for food each day and the Serbs going door-to-door looking for men to kill and women to rape. Sitting on the couch in the building vacant of people and the smell of gunpowder and burnt wafting in the air, they say they are the lucky ones.

• • •

IRC headquarters is in an abandoned building complex on the edge of town. Samantha Klein sits at a cluttered desk surrounded by boxes and dust. She's distracted by the many things she has to do and half-listens as I explain who I am. She tells me that she can help me in getting around and seeing what I need to see and even with a place to stay here in Gjilane. When I come out of the office, an Albanian man with large shoulders, thinning hair, and an IRC credential pinned to his jacket sits on the stoop. He chews on a stick spitting out the pieces.

He has noticed Junus waiting in the car outside the gate.

How much do you pay your driver?

I tell him.

And what does he do?

I tell him, so far mostly drive.

Does he show you the destroyed villages, where the people live in the tents?

I tell him, not yet.

Isn't that what you want to see?

I tell him, it is.

I can show you.

Junus stands outside the gate looking at the job board. He pulls hard at the cigarette in his mouth, his dark eyes darker, more hooded than usual.

I have just heard, he says, exhaling long and slow, they have taken my cousin from his village on the border.

Who took him?

The Serbs. They say he did things.

I'm sorry. Listen, Junus, I am going to stay here, in Gjilane, with the IRC. There is a man who knows the villages, he's going to show me.

He takes the cigarette from his mouth. You do not need me anymore?

No, I'm sorry.

He looks around at the buildings and the razor wire and the gate that goes up and down whenever one of the IRC people go out in an SUV.

Do you think these people can give me work?

I don't know, I say, and we shake hands and Junus drives off slowly.

. . .

In a Serb village high in the hills, Artan rolls down his window and asks a man hoeing his garden, do you know the way to Gadis? The man looks and points the way further down the road, in the direction we are heading, which Artan already knows. Rolling his window back up, he flashes a grin and guns the engine, I only wanted to ask him in Albanian.

The road is barely passable because of the tanks and buses that had come through a few months back, as the Serbs drove the countryside killing people. Sometimes we stop to look for a route and Artan picks his way around the potholes made by artillery shells and wash outs and eventually we descend into a picturesque valley dotted with homes that were once but now lie crumbled beside tents that say *UNHCR*.

He negotiates for me to stay several days in the village and the village elder says over tea that, this is fine, that it is their honor. He assigns one of his sons to watch over me but explains they are very busy with their annual harvest, having fallen behind because of the time they spent hiding in the forest.

Dinner that evening is served by the women who cook the food over a fire and walk it to where the men sit cross-legged on a section of floor in one of the homes still standing. With no doors and only half a roof, we wrap in blankets for warmth. Frail Halit shivers from the cold and apologizes for using an extra blanket. He speaks English learned in Australia, starting and ending his sentences with Mate. As the meal arrives, bowls of rice, potatoes, yogurt, and bread, he speaks of the days on the sheep farm, and of the beautiful weather of Australia, and of the pressures he felt to return to his village to help his people with the yearly harvest. It was many years ago, and he always thought he would return one day, but then the problems came and then the war, and now he is old and speaks only of making it through the winter. He apologizes again for complaining of the troubles of his life. Holding up a cup of water he gives a toast. Well mate, sank you for tis food you give us, tis food is your food, sank you USA, sank you mate.

We eat with our hands, dipping them into bowls and stuffing mouths, our eating shadows thrown onto the walls by the light of a bare bulb glowing off a car battery. In the shadows flits a young boy. He slips between the men to discard the empty bowls from off the floor, never taking his green eyes from the stranger. They are large eyes and young eyes and old too because they are eyes that saw the tranquility of village life, and so he knew that, but they have also seen the buses of Arkan's Tigers rolling through the pass from another world, and they are eyes that watched as the killing began, and the burning began, one house at a time, close and closer, that saw as his family took the few things they could and ran into the hills ahead of the Serbs, where they hid like rats, and when they ran out of food they ate bark from the trees and leather from their shoes.

• • •

He follows me each day, finding me in the afternoon after his schooling. When he comes upon me, he smiles in a shy manner and drops to my side, and when I move on, he moves on with me. When I set out to cross the valley for another destroyed village, he sees where I am going and runs ahead, leading the way, checking frequently over his shoulder to make sure I follow in good shape. In a village three from his own he knows someone and they call out his name and wave and he waves back and yells out who I am. When I find a place that sells sodas and cookies, I buy two each and we sit outside against a wall. With winter coming there is urgency in the village and it moves past at high speed. We talk about dreams. The little boy says he has one. He wishes to one day receive a new bicycle, and that is his dream.

*July 20, 2006*
*Jamaica Plain, Massachusetts*

Today I received an email from Matt Conway in Abeche. "Help, Confusion" was the subject. He said he needed clarification on exactly who we worked for. He said our letters were confusing. I guess that was the idea. The letter I'd written even I found hard to follow. Now he wants a clearer one, plus a copy in French.

This stresses me and I write back to Matt reiterating that I work for myself but have affiliations with an international photo agency who will take my work and sell it piecemeal to whoever wants it, or I'll sell it off daily to the wire side, if they're interested, but most likely not this time because *these are the ones that are going to survive.* I let him know it sounds odd but that's how it works. Then I run my letter through a translation website, print it, sign it, photograph it along with the passport photos, and send it back to Matt as jpegs. Sorry for the confusion, thanks for the help, I write him. If for whatever reason we are denied paperwork, our trip is dead.

## Resignation Amid Swirling Clouds of Dust and Potted Plants

The guy schedules a press conference for Thursday. He's had all week to resign. Governor Romney has been calling for his head, filing lawsuits with high-powered law firms doing pro bono work, but he decides to make the announcement Thursday. I've never liked working Thursdays. I consider it the start of my weekend, Thirsty Thursday, and today the featured event at my weekly gaming club, known as Club Birchbrow, is bean-bag toss. So it's ninety-seven degrees out and the press corps stands around panting on a stretch of shade less dirt to ironically be known one day as The Greenway. Miffed Big Dig workers move Payloaders and re-bar, and Chairman Amorello's flak, Mariellen Burns, pauses from her presser preparations. With moisture in her eyes, she remarks that, it's only right it's being done here. She wears Elton John sunglasses and a blue seamless cut at the knee, and the hardhats appraise her while she fidgets around the podium. Burns is known for never returning a phone call: and those long legs the union guys were getting a good look at. She too is like the boss; never sick on the job and never taking time off, having herself accrued several thousand dollars in unused sick and vacation pay since arriving at the Turnpike a full year before. She places several six-inch high plants behind the podium, meant to fill in the background. Like Jackie Kennedy at her husband's funeral, she looks as if her world had just fallen in. Turnpikers knock over the ankle-high bushes, trampling them in attempts to be directly behind the podium. The press inhales dust and the union workers watch with looks of amusement and contempt.

Amorello arrives, making the walk from the street, where his car drops him, through the dirt of the Greenway to the podium. He pauses to gather his thoughts, pinching his nose between fingers, and with a cracking voice begins speaking of the death of Milena Del Valle and of his years aboard the helm of the largest transportation project in the history of the United States. Of the future, he does not know what it brings, or what he will do after February next year when a government mandate rules he stop receiving his two hundred and twenty three thousand dollar a year salary. A gasp arises from the minions behind, but he holds his chin high, breaks not a tear, and thanks everyone for everything. He God blesses this great project, hopes to build again one day, and through the dust and workers, past potted plants and applauding Turnpikers, backhoes and Port-A-Johns, to the street of unknown he walks. The press follows, scurrying around each other, chasing with cameras rolling, photographers shooting, TV reporters yelling, and boom mikes dangling.

In the street, eleven-year old Billy from San Antonio walks with his mother from Faneuil Hall to the North End for some pizza. The media spectacle envelops them, and from the center steps Amorello. Billy looks up at him, squinting his eyes against the mid-day sun. He asks, can I get a picture? Amorello bends down on one knee and puts an arm around Billy from Texas and begins his resignation speech all over again, informing young Bill of just how great a project the Big Dig is and how diligent all the men and women are who've been working it these past fourteen years. He speaks of determination and courage and his eyes dampen. Billy's mother holds up a disposable point-and-shoot and takes two steps back. She clicks the picture. Amorello runs an eye over his domain one last time, and with that he is gone. The media scatters. It's mentioned to Billy, someday you will be able to say you've met Chairman Amorello. Billy says, who's that?

*July 31, 2006*
*Jamaica Plain, Massachusetts.*

I need to check on the status of my passport and visa. I sent it out two weeks ago to Travel Document Systems, an expedition company in Washington, D.C. I purchased my ticket last week, twenty-six hundred and change, but of my visa application, I'm nervous because of all the letters I faked. Malcolm and I sent in our paperwork at the same time, and he tells me that his passport came back last week. I wait four more days before calling, telling myself everything is fine, that no one gets shut out of *third world countries*.

The woman from TDS takes my name and I hear her tapping on a computer causing my tamped down fears to spike. She starts to speak, then stops, goes back to typing on the keyboard. Why would she do that? What would make her begin to say my name and stop and start typing again?

Sear?

You mean 'sir?'

Yes sear.

And now I know they have me. No one calls me Sear. They call me Daryl, Derrick, Danon, but never Sear. That's why she went back to typing. Sear, your passport has been flagged. Seems the handwriting on the visa application matches the handwriting on the letter from your editor. Also, when we called the number you put down for your employer, your father answered. Your application is being reviewed.

They weren't going to let me in. Deny me. Put the black mark in my passport and I'd be out three thousand dollars not to mention the humiliation all over again. I become panicky and dry-mouthed. I'm about to hang up when the TDS woman finishes her typing. Sear, you received your extra pages. Now your passport is in Chad for visa.

Relief strikes me. I say, great, what?

She repeats what I heard, that my passport is in Chad getting a visa.

It's actually in Chad. You sent it to Chad?

Yes sear.

Why?
Because you applied for a visa.
Yes, but maybe you mean my passport is at the Chad embassy in D.C?
Yes, it's in Chad Embassy?
Chad Embassy, D.C., not Chad Embassy Chad? And I got my visa and pages?
Yes, you received extra pages and visa for Chad today.
That's great, thank you, and you're going to send it to me?
Yes sear, it will be sent today.

## Denied Leave To Enter

When I landed at Gatwick I knew Ray would have taken the morning off from work and would be waiting for me outside customs. I'd told him he didn't have to come, that I'd take the train, but he felt it was his duty to pick me up. He'd be anxious about the missed hours at the shop and his boss not liking it, but either way, he'd come. I met Ray when he and Brian Buchanan came to Los Angeles from London so Brian could break into bodybuilding. They moved into the apartment in Palms with Ron and me. Ray trained Brian at Gold's Gym in Venice that summer. They'd go to the supermarket once a week and buy all the chickens. That's what they ate, and boiled potatoes and rice. At the end of the summer Brian did a show and placed second, and offers came in and interviews with magazines and money, and he left for Australia to open a gym. Ray went back to Hackney and the butcher shop on Seven Sisters Road.

I was only passing through London on my way to meet some friends in Austria. I'd spent the summer working back at the maintenance shack at Keene State, a job I've had on and off since I was fifteen. And I was only in New

Hampshire for the summer because of a nasty turn I'd taken that winter in an avalanche chute on Berthoud Pass in Colorado. I landed it but two days later doubled over at work fixing ski boots. When I came to, fat people from the mid-west were standing over me asking, you gonna be able to fix ma bewt by mownin? It took five hours in blizzard conditions for the ambulance to get me to the hospital in Denver with the EMT's calling in saying Code Red even as I pleaded with them to stop saying it. At the hospital I was CAT scanned and poked and stuck with needles, all the time doubled over in pain, telling anyone who would listen that I'd had a bad ski accident two days before.

The next morning, a doctor, different than the previous night's doctor, looked at my X-rays. He told me there was nothing wrong. They released me. The pain lingered. I could no longer ski. Back in Breckenridge I minded the shop, cleaning the house on days off. Every other week I'd hitchhike back to Boulder, stay overnight at a friend's house, and take a bus the next morning into Denver for another checkup. The hospital was in a rough neighborhood and that mile-long walk from the bus stop seemed longer than it was, shuffling along slow, bent at the waist, watching my shoes.

The doctors told me I was fine and that made me feel better but it did nothing for the constant tug of pain in my lower abdomen. One morning I took the five am from Boulder to Denver and made the walk to the hospital and drank a chalky substance and they ran a tube down my throat. They said they'd call to let me know. I was exhausted and the chalk stuff made me nauseous. I took a seat in the waiting room and passed out sitting up. A security guard woke me. He told me there's no sleeping in the waiting room. Through a light snow I made the shuffle walk back to the bus stop.

A doctor called. He explained I had Crohns disease and I needed to see a specialist. He said I needed to do this right away. He said Crohns is serious. I called my family and told them I had Crohn's disease and it was serious and I needed to see a specialist right away. I spent the week wondering what Crohn's disease was, doubled over at the ski shop while my co-workers got in their daily runs plus mine. At the end of the week I hitchhiked down to Boulder and took the bus into Denver and saw the specialist who asked if I'd had any accidents or taken any trauma to my mid section lately. I told him all about the thirty-foot drop off the avalanche chute where I narrowly missed the cat track and my friends thought I was dead. How they kept calling to me, but I couldn't seem to answer at first. How Matt had to side-step up and dig deep for one of my skies and how I thought I might have caught a fist in my mid-section when I landed. He said, you don't have Crohn's, you had internal bleeding, it needs time to heal. He gave me horse pills and I thanked him for telling me I didn't have Crohn's and walked back to the bus stop and took it into Boulder and walked to my friends house and called my parents and told them I didn't have Crohn's, I only had internal bleeding, it just needs time to heal. We were all relieved. When the ski season ended we took our annual end-of-ski-season road trip through the southwest desert, climbing to the bottom of the Grand Canyon and mountain biking the Slickrock Trail in Moab. Then I drove cross-country to New Hampshire to work for the summer at the maintenance shack.

When summer ended I decided to go to Europe and meet up with friends, Paul and Marco, from my Los Angeles days. I was at loose ends, wandering, looking for something and not knowing what. I wasn't a Colorado ski rat, and L.A. hadn't worked out. My hometown didn't seem to be my hometown anymore. Ray had said, come anytime mate, I can put you to work in the shop. I didn't know if I was a shop worker either but the shop was in London and that seemed a better place to spend the winter than New Hampshire, where my choice of jobs was narrowed down to what tools I knew how to use. If nothing more it would buy me time. That's what I was thinking, standing in line, waiting to pass through customs and blinking the overnight flight from my head, when a man taps me on the shoulder. He says, sit there. I look to where he points and wonder why he wants me specifically to sit in that plastic chair. He seemed sure he wants me, and not the guy behind me, or the woman in front, and they were also on my plane. From the plastic chair I watch the line shorten and, as it does, my stomach tightens and the people are called to the customs booth and answer simple questions, passing through the doors into the United Kingdom. Suddenly I am conscious of my clothes. I wear Dunham work boots. So do every guy and half the women I grew up with, but so do laborers. My grey Keene State College sweatshirt is cut at the forearms, my hair is long, and the only bag I carry is the knapsack over my shoulder with two pairs of jeans, some underwear, socks, and T-shirts.

I feel panic and urge myself to stay calm. I want to go back out and come in again, start over. No one tells me what to do next and I sit in the now-empty customs area. More people arrive from another plane and I briefly consider getting back in line. It's fine. Everything's fine, I repeat. But I know it is not because this is not the first time this has happened.

Sue and I had flown into the U.K three years before. Sue's a second year nursing student at Northeastern. She's got money, an itinerary, and a proper reason for being there. I'd quit my construction job at A1 Builders and carried the one week's pay in my pocket. She wants to see Big Ben, the Colosseum, Le Louvre. I want to see her naked. We grew up together, sat a desk apart in homeroom throughout junior high and high school. In junior high she was gangly, in high school curvy, and by the time we landed in Europe, I would have quit my job for her in a moments notice and taken all the money I had and followed her anywhere she said. Now I too am interested in the paintings of El Greco and Renaissance architecture.

For her it was a temporary break from college, but I had intentions on staying and had flown in on a one-way ticket. I had three hundred dollars in cash and a five-hundred dollar limit credit card co-signed by my father. Sue gets called to the customs counter first, and she's young and looks the part of the college sabbatical traveler. She shows her passport, answers questions, and gets her first stamp. She smiles over to me holding up her passport. Cool, I smile back, that easy. I step to the counter. The customs man looks at me and I continue the smile because he hasn't smiled back yet and I wait for the same simple questions Sue got and the same cool stamp. Where do you live? California. Where are you coming from? There. What's you're purpose for coming? Travel? Who do you know in London? Ray. Where do you plan on staying? Rays. Do you plan on working? What? I did the best I could but I was shaky and my answers even to me sounded shady. He kept popping the questions: duration of stay? two or three weeks- reason for travel? see things.

Sue glares from the doorway, waiting for me, mouthing come on, and I can tell she's worried which makes me worried and I fidget in front of the man, feeling guilty. I try to concentrate, to remember my answers in case he revisits the questions. He seems hung up on my one-way ticket and what he sees as a lack of money. I say for the third time, I'm with her, pointing to Sue, like it's helping, and just when I'm about to cry in front of the customs man, he slams the cool stamp into my passport.

So now, sitting in the plastic chair, I prepare my answers and tell myself that this time is like that time only this time I have an open-ended ticket and two credit cards. I have been through this before. It's procedure. I shake my insecurity and wait. A man in uniform approaches and instructs me to follow him. I stand up, looking over my shoulder to the empty customs area waiting for the next planeload of travelers, and follow the man through a door that he opens with a key.

He leads me to a cell like structure and tells me to wait inside. It's "cell" because it has bars and locks from the outside and because men stand on the other side of the bars and watch the people on the inside of the bars, but it's "like" because there is a vending machine, pay phone, two rooms, benches and chairs.

This didn't happen before. This is bad. There are other people in the cell and although they are better dressed they look as if they have done something wrong. Silently I berate myself for not putting on a nice pair of chinos yesterday.

As time passes, the cell grows smaller. I begin worrying for Ray. By now he knows something is wrong. He might think I missed the plane, but he won't leave the airport until he knows for sure. He must be looking at his watch, needing to get back to work. A thick-set man sticks his head into the cell and instructs me to follow a thin-set man and I end up in a windowless, cinderblock room, walls painted a faint yellow.

Good day, says the thin man, squinting at a document he holds in his hand. My heart begins to race, wondering where they'd gotten a document on me. They had taken my passport, asked a few questions, and now they had a document. Thin man continues to use my last name and says, down his even thinner nose, we're a bit concerned as to why you have asked leave to enter the country?

I'm looking him in the eye and trying, but those words do not make sense and I realize then I'm tired and not ready for what I see now as the coming long haul.

No sir. I don't want leave. I want stay.

You're well into your twenties correct?

Not well, but, mid-way, yes.

And you are not currently enrolled in University, nor have you completed one?

College? I was in one before I came. And I said it with pride, referring to my almost two years of collective credits from Keene State and Santa Monica City College. I was about to point out that both of those colleges rate tops among their kind when he interrupts me.

And it appears you currently have no job?

Now phrased as such, it becomes a difficult answer. I try to explain that since I am here and traveling, no, I don't currently have a job, that I have a job later when I return, yes-but once he hears the word no he stops listening and bends over his document and writes with his twiggy hand. I try to look and feel a sweat breaking. I am desperate for sleep and maybe some food. The three beers on the plane last night are causing me heartburn. I babble, I left it, I mean, my job, to come here, I have a job, I just have to go and get it back again, in California, I was just in New Hampshire for the summer, I'm travelling for a while now, from here to Paris and Austria, to see friends, so I just left my job for a little while.

But I talk to the top of his bald head. When he's finished with his notes he slides a pad of paper and pen to me and says, write down the history of your life from high school graduation to this day. With no further instruction he leaves the room. What did he mean by history, exactly? Dates? Major events? Does he want specifics or just a round up? I feel fear and then anger and then panic. One minute I'm going to tear up the pad of paper and wait for his thin ass to return, tell him fuck off ain't writing no history, and the next minute I despair and if his thin ass might return he'll find me forehead on the table weeping gently.

My head spins and the room falls in but I breathe deep through my nose. I fight the insecurity. Pull it together. Just some silly shit to deal with. I'll laugh this off later at a pub in Hackney. But I was starting not to believe that.

It takes me a while to remember what I'd done since high school graduation, June 1985. I work diligently for the hour and going over it smile at the things I'd been able to achieve so far in life, for not many people had hiked the Grand Canyon top to bottom twice or skied one hundred days in a season twice or driven cross country and lived in California and Colorado twice. I saw it as a well-traveled and diverse story, rich in adventure.

Thin man enters the room, picks up my work, reads.

Says you've dropped out of two universities, and had, his finger traces words in my history statement, nine jobs. That right sir?

Or, taken another way, my history could be seen as a total waste of time.

That's right-are you sure nine jobs? *I should have edited.*

Where did you grow up?

Ah, says right there, first paragraph, Keene, New Hampshire.

Went to the local university?

College. Yes sir.

Then you quit and left to go skiing in Vail? He speaks the sentence like he doesn't approve.

No. I quit university AFTER I left to go skiing in Vail. And I got in over a hundred days that year. Also in the report.

Wonderful. So let me clarify. In the United States, you can come and go from University as you like?

Yes, we can do whatever we want in the United States. Can I talk to my friend now? He's waiting for me. I must have some rights, don't I? What did I do exactly?

I was trying to keep it together, to be patient, but it had been hours and the lack of food wasn't helping. Nor did it help that before they'd separated me from the others I'd watched several of my shady-looking pen mates get allowed into the country. Me they have writing out memoirs, but that guy from Jammu, it's a snapshot and a welcome to the U.K.

I knew they'd spoken with Ray, because I knew what it was now, and I knew the questions they would ask him and how they'd do it. They'd see him with his thick hands and weathered face and they would know they could bully him, and Ray would be nervous because Ray was always nervous around people, much less official people. He was too simple for most things and certainly this. They would press him. Was he gonna work for you-Raymond? What Ray must have thought when they approached him without warning, waiting in the terminal, thinking I'd be out any second. Instead, a tap on the shoulder, excuse me sir, could you come with us a minute. He must have near died. It was killing me to think he would have to say yes sir no sir to these assholes, stuttering it out, all because of me.

After you left the second university-

It was a city college, not a university.

Yes. And for what reason did you leave city college?

Went to live in Colorado with the same guys I lived with the other time I left college to go skiing. I left because the acting wasn't working out, Los Angeles sucked. I left, Jesus man, its all there, third page.

They let me see Ray for a few minutes outside the cinderblock room with the yellow walls. He looked as nervous as I thought he would, and tired, because he gets up early for work. He whispers they asked him some strong questions but he'd said nothing about me working. I know he wonders what I've said. He stares and picks the black from under his finger nails and glances at his watch and a man says it's time for him to go. He shakes my hand and says, sorry mate, I'm really sorry. I tell him he owes me no apologies and that I'll see him someday. Before he leaves he speaks of missing Los Angeles and that he thinks of it often. Pulling seventeen-hour days six days a week at the butcher shop, I'll bet he does.

Back in my cinderblock room, my moods swing. I tell myself it's my own fault, that I was getting what I deserved, that if I had wanted I could have worn a collared shirt and better shoes and I'd be in the West End by now. But this was always my way. Flaunting it with long hair and bracelets. Did you do your homework, young man? Yes. Where is it? Home. Why is it not here? You only said do it, not bring it. They said that attitude would get me nowhere. This was it. This was what they meant. A cell in stupid Gatwick getting thrown out of a country I was only passing through.

Then, the hell with it, I was a fine young man. What care was it of theirs how I lived my life and what my credit card limit was? So what if I thought Dunham's and blue jeans were proper travel attire? If they didn't want me, then I would just go on to Paris and Austria and fuck them, so whatever customs asshole there was needed to come and deliver me their verdict. I have the speeches with myself, muttering them up against the wall like a prisoner in solitary. The door opens and in comes a man different from the thin man before.

Hello sir.

You guys are older than me but you call me sir. What's going on, where's Twiggy?

Sir, I've had a chance to review your history here, as well as your entry card, and I would just like to ask you one question. Before you came here, you worked at a "maintenance shack"?

Yes. I told the other guy that, plus I wrote it all down. Where'd he go?

His shift ended. How old are you sir?

Well into my twenties.

Sir, do you have plans to work in this country?

No. I told you in the history report. I am meeting my friend Ray who I know from when he came to stay with me in my country, the United States. Then I'm heading to Vienna to meet up with Marco and Paul, also in the report. I'm only passing through this country.

He says, we do believe that you are here to work illegally and we have decided to deny you leave to enter.

What?

You're being denied leave to enter.

Does that mean I can come in or not?

We'll be flying you back to Boston.

It didn't help when I told him I didn't live in Boston. He said, you flew in from Boston and that's where we are flying you back to. He ignored the insults about fish and chips and bad weather and led me down the hallway back to the holding pen.

Three hours later, portly men carrying sticks encircle me and I am walked through the terminal to the gate. All the people waiting in line for the overnight to Boston watch as the dangerous man with long hair and work boots is led onto the plane, surrounded by the men with sticks. When they board moments later they file to their seats sneaking peeks out of the corners of their eyes. They watch as the stewardess approaches the man and as the plane taxis down the runway she hands to him a passport. They watch as he gestures for her to come closer, and hear him say, gimme a whiskey, sweets, but what the stewardess heard was, could you please get me a ginger ale and some chips, I'm so hungry.


*August 1, 2006*
*Jamaica Plain, Massachusetts*
*21 days to go*

Yesterday Cathy called. She was at my father's, where my grandmother is staying while he's away in Turkey. It's all part of the routine for the Drake neighbors, who, when they see Leslie at my father's after he has gone traveling ask, when's Gram coming? Same as when my dad departs: Grammy moves in behind Leslie moments after she and her family leave for the airport. And my father still has not figured out why no one ever wonders or seems to care when he's returning from his travels.

Grammy likes Dad's Barcalounger, which she calls Barky, where she can sit and rock and look out the plate glass window at the ocean and watch *Law and Order* reruns. The ocean view, the crashing waves, the green lawns; it all beats the elderly housing complex in Keene.

There has been a heat wave. Cathy explains Grammy called my mother at work to say she had not been feeling well and perhaps if she didn't feel better later in the week could she get a ride to the hospital? This runs in the family. If it had been my father, or my stepfather, my mother probably would have said, sure, let me know how you feel. But this was Gram and she's ninety and unlike others in the family, she doesn't complain incessantly, and so my mother called Cathy and told her to go check it out.

Cathy said it took Grammy a long time to open the door and she was slurring her words. She called 9-1-1. The medics came and rushed her to the hospital. She was dehydrated and run down and hadn't been eating well, not drinking enough water, and, also, so as not to run up the electric bill, she'd not been using the air-conditioner. Gram also tells my mother and Cathy, when they visit her later that night, that she's been a little stressed lately because a few days before Donny was diagnosed with a double aortic aneurism. That's her other son, my Dad's brother, my uncle.

I Googled it. An aortic aneurism is a bulge in a blood vessel much like a bulge in an over-inflated inner tube. Aneurysms are dangerous because they can burst at any time, spilling blood outside of the aorta and leaving a person at risk for hemorrhaging within the abdominal cavity. They can be hereditary. I emailed Sue to inquire about the hereditary part and she's vague in her reply, mentioning it can skip generations. She is clear on one thing, they are not good.

Grammy was hesitant to tell anyone about this and doesn't say why, but it's because of the time my father traveled to San Francisco when his father was sick, and he died while away. Grammy's probably thinking that, doesn't want to upset my father during his travels, nothing he can do anyway, by making that call. Uncle Donny's going in for emergency surgery and even though they don't talk much he had sent out an email to Dad saying he should see a doctor, because of it being hereditary. Now everyone is riled up saying Dad needs to get checked immediately, and me too. If my father has it then he will have to go into the hospital for emergency surgery and my chances of having it become more likely. I don't want my father to have this, because I don't want to have this. I'm going to Chad soon. I can't have a double aortic aneurism.

That night I stay up until one am and call my father at his hotel in Barcelona. I know what he's going to be thinking when he hears my voice. I'd think it too.

Hola?

Hola Dad.

Son?

I jump right in and give it to him all at once. He knows I'm not calling to see how his trip went. I didn't even know he was in Barcelona until Cathy explained he'd gone there to visit Leslie on his way back from Turkey.

Listen, just needed to call you and let you know that Uncle Donny has been diagnosed with a double aortic aneurism and he's going into the hospital for emergency surgery and also Grammy got heat stroke and the paramedics came to your apartment and rushed her to the hospital. She stills there, she's fine, just dehydrated, its' been real hot. Donny says an aortic aneurysm is hereditary, maybe your Dad had it, and that you may have it too and you need to get checked when you get back. He sent you an email. So how was Turkey?

He told stories of the markets and bazaars of Istanbul and how he loved hummos and Muslims and listening to the evening call to prayer while watching sunsets fade to night drinking thick coffees in outdoor cafés. He told me how he filled two moleskin notebooks with writing and of the pictures he took and how he's already planning another trip to the Middle East. He's sixty-four. For several generations no men on my fathers side of the family have lived past sixty-seven. My grandfather Ed set that mark. My mother's father died of cancer around the time I was born. Uncle Donny had his first stroke in his early fifties. He doesn't exercise much beyond hunting and fishing, his cholesterol is perfect, and still he had the stroke. My Dad hikes, bikes, and goes to the gym five times a week. His cholesterol is sky-high and he's on Lipitor. Earlier this year, Uncle Bob Callahan, fire chief of Keene, passed away at the age of eighty-six. There was a state funeral for him and we all marched from Foley Funeral Home with a procession of firefighters past the firehouse and down Main Street to St. Bernard's Church where he and my Aunt Evelyn were married fifty-six years before. It was the first family funeral since Grampa Ed's, when his high school football coach leaned over me in front of the casket and I could smell his aftershave, to tell me how fine a player Grampa was, and Grampa was always big and strong and carried a gun and went fishing and now he was in a box and my father was crying and I'd never seen him cry. When no one was looking I slipped out the back door and ran to the alley where I found aimless Rodney smoking cigarettes and that's where I stayed until the funeral ended and they yelled for me.

The memories run through my head as my father talks on about his travels and I tune him out thinking about my own upcoming trip: age, mine and his: emergencies: getting hurt: dying: death. It's late, way past bedtime, and that's what happens when you stay up and think too much.

Twenty-one and waiting for a flight out of Manchester Airport, Ron recently out of jail and not knowing exactly where in California Los Angeles is, north or south. What he knows, it's hot year-round and he's psyched to get the fuck out of Keene. He's going to be a stunt man and me an actor. Whatever. Getting out is getting out. No more small-town shit. No more fist fights and DUI's and cheating sluts who fuck your best friends and worst enemies.

I'm beginning to nod and I cut Dad off. He's still on a high, still in a hotel in Barcelona, talking about Istanbul and travel and how great it all is. He says he'll do what he has to when he gets back and not to worry because there's nothing we can do until then. He says, buenos noches.

## The Discriminating Traveler

In Hartford there is one hotel that presents luxury class hospitality preferred by discriminating travelers, and that's The Goodwin. It offers an experience of poise without pretense and has been voted Hartford's "Best Hotel" for it's elegant accommodations and impeccable service. Luxury-class stuff and poise without pretense is surely important in the choosing of a hotel room, but the word *discriminating* does bother me. Still, I had called around to some other hotels to find them booked, while The Goodwin had one room left, so I overlooked the discrimination aspect and focused on the elegant accommodations and impeccable service, booking the room for two nights at one-eighty nine a night.

U.S Senator Joe Lieberman, just months ago, seemed a sure thing for another term in office until a Kennedy-looking guy named Ned Lamont decided to run against him. Lamont had been doing a good job of tying Lieberman to President Bush and Iraq and what with it being summer, people weren't talking about the war so much, less "Ra-Ra bring it on." What had once seemed an easy primary win for Lieberman now had him fighting for his political life. His people were trying to remain upbeat in the face of sagging poll numbers. They said his victory speech would be delivered in Hartford at The Goodwin Hotel on the night of August eighth.

I do the two-hour drive down to Connecticut with the windows open and pull off the highway in a sweat. It's over ninety degrees outside but my heater blasts on high and I can feel water dripping down my legs, pooling in the small of my back making my skin itch against the car seat. I need to run the heater in summer to keep the engine from overheating. Though on the upside, the '89 Honda Accord is great on gas.

In the parking garage I shoulder my bags and walk to the entrance past a foreign man with a bushy mustache working the garage checkout. Inside, workers measure out a stage for tomorrow night's event. Struggling with my bags, the air-conditioned cool hits me and I go from hot to freeze. I get goose bumps and my nuts disappear into the lower part of my stomach. My shirt is twisted across my chest from the camera bag strap and my computer bag dangles from my overstretched left hand fingers. Behind me, my clothes bag drags on rollers that hang up each time I turn a corner.

The check-in lady speaks with the bellhop. He leans against the baggage rack and she says, oh honny where you go dis weekend wif your girl? Oh don't dat soun fawn. There is no notice taken of me and I stand, wanting to say something, to clear my throat, but I'm aware of the whole discriminating traveler issue and wish not to offend anyone. No, I'll wait. They'll finish their conversation in good time. Even with all last night's sleep the energy today is off and I know that whatever I say, excuse me, do you see me standing here in front of you with all this luggage? will only come out sounding, hey snap-to-it you lazy black bastards, I'm holding bags. I like luxury and class and poise but I'm not into that. This place is known for its impeccable service, says so right on the website, so I stand and wait for it.

The check-in lady with the smooth accent concludes the bellhop, likes ada women too mush, and her head is down to her desk and bellhop nods and strolls off down the way. Just to be sure, I run my hand across my eyes.

Hello.

The check-in lady looks up as if she's heard a noise and can't quite place it. She peers around trying to find the source. When she sees nothing, she sees me. Yes good day. How may I help you?

Wondering in how many ways she possibly thinks she could help, I say, pointing to the sign, I'd like to check in. I give her my name and she repeats it and is all business now and I regret my low-blood sugar racist thoughts. Impeccably she punches the keys on her computer and says, yes sir right here, and speaks my name again and I tell her, that's me, got the last one huh, busy week, and she looks at me. She hands me a room key, sis two nine, top floah.

The bell hop who likes ada women is nowhere to be seen and the check-in lady is finished with me, so I shoulder my bags and go off to find the elevator. I walk for a time, maybe not an hour but it feels like an hour, what with all the bags and the whole hot-freeze thing going on and the lack of food, and eventually I see two elevators. I choose the first one and get in, looking to press the number six, finding no number six. The other elevator is in use and I wait until it returns and the door dings open. Chuckling, I step in and reach to press the number six but again it's not there. Like the other one this elevator too seems only to go to five. I count all the little glowing buttons, one two three four five, no six. I get out and look at the numbers above the elevator doors and they too stop at five. Walking into the hallway I see nothing but the walls and the atrium where the workers build the stage. Getting into the first elevator again, I look harder for the number six and still it is not there. I punch the five button, deciding to see what will happen, figuring that the six-hundred rooms on the fifth floor must be part of that classic turn-of-the-century motif that combines with the turn-of-the-millennium convenience. Sixes on five? Way more convenient.

The first room I come to on the fifth floor has a five hundred number on the door. I walk the hall one way, then the other, shifting my bags from shoulder to shoulder to ease the growing pinch in my neck. I look at all the numbers as I walk, one room at a time, to be sure they didn't put my room, six twenty nine, in between five twenty eight and five thirty. It's not there also.

The elevator is gone. I jab my finger into the down button over and over but it takes its time, mocking me with dings from two floors below. During the wait I talk with the elevator door and tell it what I think of it and it's stupid millennium ways. Ding. Screw you.

I stalk to the front desk as best I can but, with all the cumbersome bags I find it difficult to properly show my irritation, and at the lobby my roller bag catches the corner and I enter into a most fierce fight with it, yanking it free and flinging it across the floor. My shirt is twisted about my neck, and, as if in a fever, I'm sweating and chilled to the bone. The playboy bellhop leans against the luggage rack watching as if I bore him. The check-in lady looks up from her desk at the sounds of the commotion. Yes sir, how may I help you?

Room six two nine? You just checked me in. Where is it?

Take elevator to top floah.

No no. I just did that. You only have five floors.

Oh dear I am so sorry, and she breaks into a hearty Caribbean laugh where its like whatever is wrong in the world can be fixed with an afternoon mai tai. Oh honny, I shoulda explain to you bettah. You need to go pass the first set a elevators pass the stairway to the lass set of elevators on the left and take that un to the top floah.

That one has the sixes?

Yes dear, that'll have the sixes.

Her head is back down to her desk and the playboy bellhop lollygags idle and I ignore my discrimination fears snapping, shouldn't you have told me that when I first checked in, just go past the first set of elevators to the second set of elevators. Couldn't you have said that fifteen minutes ago? I just walked around the fifth floor and rode both elevators and I've checked in twice now and what's that guy's job? Is it to help guests with their bags? Cause I've got those.

She sees me now, recognizes me, registers the overheated state I am in. My voice echoes around the cavernous lobby in a shrill pitch that even I can hear is dangerously close to losing it. Suddenly she's snapping her fingers and the playboy bellhop reaches quickly for my roller bag and places it on his golden luggage rack but when he reaches for my camera bag I slap his hand away.

We ride the elevator together in silence. Taking from me my room key, he opens the door and, because the room is so small, we jockey around each other in the little hallway, ass-to-ass. Inside the room it's dark, even after the lights are turned on. I part the curtains to see a brick building six feet away, ensuring the darkness. Playboy bellhop stands in the hallway smiling. I walk to him and, at the door, smile back before closing it in his face.

An hour later I'm on the street looking for a restaurant. I need food. I come to the Trumbull Kitchen. Reading the menu, the food looks average and I'm about to keep on when a sinewy young waitress approaches. She has the striking feel of a cheerleader. I ask for the window seat. I want a newspaper and go into the street to find one. Inserting coins into a machine I hear and see some college kids handing out flyers at the intersection. Their signs say "GO JOE." One young man hands me a flyer and turns to scream *GO JOE* at a passing car. The leaflet says come visit with Joe at Vito's By The Park this evening at five. The young man sweats heavily and I ask him why he's doing this, out handing flyers on such a hot summer day. He wipes his face with his shirtsleeve, leaving wet marks on the cuff. He supports Lieberman's policies, he's into politics, Lieberman's a friend of the family.

At the restaurant I'm thumbing through the paper when I hear a voice ask, what can I get you? I look up to see another waitress, who looks to be a teammate of the other waitress on the college cheerleading squad. Her collar is low-cut and reveals a bright-red that-morning hicky. Whoever did it was a righty biter, leaving perfect teeth indentations circling a bloody welt on the left side of her neck, just below the chin. I ask for the menu again in order to point out the Cobb salad, to be sure I don't accidently order a bright-red-that-morning hicky. I become fixated and try not to stare. I point to the item on the menu and she says, great, be right back with your drink. She returns with my iced tea and leans across the table, and no matter how hard I try, look left, look right, it can't be helped. Her golden delicious swing freely in my direction and I feel a tickle somewhere in my belly and find myself leaning forward, mouth open, hands reaching, when she says with a smile, be right back with your salad. Twenty minutes later after picking at my lunch I leave a forty percent tip and head to Vito's.

Brian Snyder is sitting in his car talking on a cell phone, making hotel plans for New Haven tonight. Brian is with Reuters. He's also based in Boston. We compete fiercely to get our photos onto the wire first, and we would do almost anything in this regard, but if there is one thing we have an alliance on, it is to beat the Associated Press. He calls them The Apes.

He says he's staying the night in New Haven because Lieberman votes there in the morning, at a school near his home. I'll have to get up that much earlier and drive, but it's a tradeoff with the convention in town, and needing a room tomorrow night as well. Brian was going to have to stay somewhere else or drive back to Boston after tomorrow's event because there were no more rooms at the Goodwin, me getting the last one.

A white-haired elderly man stands on the corner waiting for the senator to arrive in a bus called Joe's Tomorrow Tour. He holds a "Vote Joe" sign and wears a T-shirt that reads, "I'm Sticking with Joe." When the bus pulls up, he waves the sign and the senator steps out and the old guy and the few others and the flyer-handing college students scream *Go Joe* to the passing cars that slow to look and honk their horns. Senator Chris Dodd and Representative John Larson pull Lieberman onto the brownstone stoop next door to the restaurant, urging him to make a speech. He waves his hand around in the air saying he feels good but it's apparent he had nothing written for the occasion. Then he goes into Vito's By The Park, where he shakes hands with bewildered eaters halfway through the shellfish sampler. My credentials hang from my neck over a woman's plate as I lean across her table to take a photo. Pardon me. Click. Is that the lobster ravioli? And the senator tells a table of well-dressed elderly picking at a beef Carpaccio why he's best suited to represent them in Congress, while the woman confirms it is indeed lobster ravioli, and declares it just delicious. I tell her, sure does smell that way, and afterwards order it to go and eat it that night in room six two nine of The Goodwin Hotel.

## Running with the Senator

It's a forty-five minute drive to New Haven but I take no chances and early is good. Flat tires, wrong turns, overheating cars, too many things can go wrong and not getting there means not getting paid. So just after seven the next morning I grab a coffee from the hotel lobby and head to my car in the parking garage. I want to be at Edgewood Magnet School in New Haven for nine thirty. Lieberman would go there in his bus, vote, exit the voting booth, flash thumbs up to assure the people he voted correctly, and then drive on to three other events before hunkering down in his suite at the Goodwin to wait out election results sometime around mid-night.

The day is as glorious as my mood and I roll down the parking garage listening to my blown muffler reverb off the concrete walls, music sweet music. The gate is closed. There is no one to be seen, no foreign man with a bushy moustache. It must go up on it's own once you wait, so I wait and idle the engine, watching the gate. There's a key card thingy. I wave my hand at it, touch it, tap on it, blow at it, and still the gate remains closed. Yanking the emergency break and getting out of the car, I walk toward the booth in a slightly less glorious mood.

Foreign man with bushy moustache has been replaced by sleeping college kid with peach fuzz. His legs are outstretched and he's mostly slumped off the stool, his head below the counter, the stool about to tip over. I yell and he moves like he's settling into a wonderful dream rather than sleeping at work and holding up the busy customer. I decide if I have to walk all the way over to wake him I'm going to tomahawk his exposed windpipe. Lets go buddy, I yell, and he snorts, pops up, coming too, laughing. He squints, rubbing sleepy seeds out of his eyes. How long you been standing there?

I give him a hand's up who cares and walk to the car and he opens the gate and I roll down to the booth and gun the engine, revving the rpm's to red, and say, thanks man through the white smoke and then David Bowie's singing about being a hero and the traffic is light and I take the highway south thinking about the day. It's a silly photo, but there's pressure in making it; making it and moving it. Lieberman steps from the voting booth after pulling the lever and *snap* it's two thumbs up. Usually that rolls around into a V and then maybe back to the thumbs or even double thumbs, but they never do a double V because of Nixon, and only the dumb ones wave.

It's simple enough but it won't come easy. The main problem would be the press itself, there'll be a lot, and the managing of how to shoot the picture of the senator getting off the bus, walking into the voting station, and getting a spot near the *correct* voting booth. Take a position in front of booth one, and candidate goes in booth three, you're done. The photo needs to be on the wire immediately too because Lieberman Lamont looks to be the day's top story. Ned Lamont is running strong in the polls and Lieberman continues talking about the war in Iraq but it's summer and the war isn't popular now and the people without money enough to go on vacation are talking about the economy and taxes and schools instead. And it's his voter base with money enough to be out of town on vacation.

There are the numerous television trucks lined up outside the school and photographers standing in the already hot sun. I recognize AP's Bob Child. He was the only other wire shooter there the day Lamont announced he would run against Lieberman back in March at the Old Statehouse in Hartford, when everybody smiled and said probably not but he sure looks Kennedy. I see Brian and a few others, camera's hanging from shoulders.

The crowd consists of supporters and handlers and staff speaking positively. They shake hands and hug. One man wears a yarmulke and hoists a sign above his head with "Jews for Lamont" on one side and "Lieberman--Worst U.S. Senator" on the other. His eyes dart edgy and angry as he moves among the pro-Lieberman crowd, looking for confrontation. He strides back and forth in a direct line, pushing through anybody in his way. He shouts Jews for Lamont into the day. His path becomes blocked and the angry Jew goes face-to-face with a Lieberman supporter: the press circles. Lieberman's people shout, go home no one wants you here hater, and the man shouts back, I have a right to be here, Jews for Lamont Jews for Lamont. The light is sharp, tough, and backlit, and the photographers test exposures by shooting flash no flash into their snarling faces, looking at the backs of their cameras to decide which is best.

Joe's Tomorrow Tour bus arrives. The press corps gathers at the door, which remains shut, and we point at it microphones and booms and TV cameras and the photographers continue to test exposures and for a while, when no one comes out, it appears our subject is the bus door itself. Then it opens and out comes Hani, Lieberman's daughter, smiling shyly, as we blast her, realizing it's not the senator, and after her comes Matt, the older son, and he gives a seasoned fist-pump and we blast him too and then Hadassah, his wife, exits the bus and my flash struggles to regenerate and that's when U.S. Senator Joseph Lieberman steps out. He's doing the thumbs-up thing already and shaking hands with supporters and smiling but it appears forced and he's not as confident looking as he might be. He wades through the jostling mob toward the school and we do the hop scotch, grabbing shots in-between and he's answering questions yelled at him from feet away, Senator how do you feel about the latest poll numbers that have you down? And he flashes thumbs-up to show how he feels.

Senator Lieberman greets the elderly women manning the voter sign-in table as the press jockeys in the background. Between the TV cameras and stills and talking heads, local and national, the grade-school gymnasium is packed. He has three booths to choose from and stands in front of the middle one and everyone tries to guess and the TV cameramen hiss, stills down front. He goes in booth number one, directly in front of where I crouch. It's shoulder-to-shoulder and quiet now as the senator is casting his vote, when along comes a photographer, having just arrived. He wants a little spot up front. He's older and heavy-set and wears a vest from which dangles every single piece of gear ever sold in a camera store. He tries to move through, saying, excuse me please, and the cameramen are on him quick, telling him to fuck off and the ball is tightened and he's pushed to the back and wants to talk it over, when out steps Lieberman.

Two decades in office on the line to a guy who months earlier decided he could do a better job, losing badly, but when he steps out from that red white and blue voting booth he looks up, smiles, and goes with a victory sign, and the cameras flash and the questions are yelled and he works the V into a thumbs-up and then comes back around to the V and then he makes for the door. The press blocks his way.

Senator, how do you feel?

Optimistic, real good, ready to continue serving-

Will you run as an independent in November if you lose today?

We're not looking beyond today, those are decisions for the future-I only said I might.

Mr. Senator, how do you feel about your chances?

Optimistic. Real Good.

Equipment bangs my hips as I run to the car. Brian and I have the same plan, to follow the senator's bus to the next two campaign events and then return to Hartford to prepare for the speech. We queue up behind the bus and turn it into a convoy with a TV truck and a reporter in a red Bronco, and I begin downloading pictures onto my computer. The bus rolls down narrow streets and I drive carefully with my knees as I move the picture of Lieberman flashing his V-sign into Photoshop and, while I'm working in curves and levels, Joe's Tomorrow Tour bus runs a yellow light. So I run the red light. A New Haven morning commuter glares but I take little notice because I'm having a bitch of a time burning down the senator's fingers. The flash really juiced and blew them out. At the next intersection, while lassoing the hot-white fingers, the senator's bus runs the red light, so I run the really red light, and while drivers slam on their breaks I knock the overexposed fingers down to acceptable levels and begin writing captions.

When we hit the highway it's a relief because I've got two photos ready to send and driving in city traffic and editing photos is difficult while driving in highway traffic and editing photos is easy. Maybe Joe runs late, I don't know, but when we hit the highway the bus driver hits the pedal and soon my car shakes as the convoy nears ninety. Brian drafts mere feet behind the bus, swerving, and I know he's editing and maybe even transmitting, and this thought stresses me.

By the time we pull off the highway, I've got four photos ready to go and the bus winds through the streets of Strafford looking for the fire station. I step from the car and walk with my computer up and down the sidewalk looking for green bars on the wireless. I see Brian hurrying to the event.

You file?

Got one out.

That was crazy. The bus driver was flying.

Flying.

In front of a yellow house is an open Wi-FI spot, and as people walk by staring with curiosity, I transmit three pictures to New York and feel relieved, because I know it's better to crash my car in a ball of flames and face a fiery death than to be late to the wire.

Lieberman stands around a table piled high with Dunkin' Donuts. There are cream-filled and jelly-filled and maple glazed. People listen, nodding, wiping powder from their cheeks. He's mentioning 9/11 and talking sacrifice and courage and ends the speech by holding up a Box O' Joe. There is a chuckle among the meager crowd. After a chocolate frosted and cream ONE sugar, we chase the bus, running red lights through town again, but this time it's less risky because there's no deadline. The driver shatters records for a Greyhound bus and I can only keep it in sight as it hits ninety-five down the highway to Shelton, pulling into a shopping plaza parking lot. There is no one there except a few old people and a woman with a little girl who holds a sign that reads, "I'm For Joe." She's cute and talkative but the sign's flimsy, written in ballpoint pen on basic white paper like she hacked it out just moments before. There is less press now and the small contingent gathers around the senator as he kneels to the little girl, and as she explains how she's supporting him for office, Brian and I head to our cars and drive a comfortable eighty miles an hour back to Hartford.

## We Want Peas

At a red light in Hartford I see Reuters' Jessica Rinaldi. She's craning her head, looking for street signs.

Lost?

Yep.

She follows me to The Goodwin. In the atrium the crews are almost finished with the stage. The last touch, a massive American flag, hanging in the background. Television crews have already marked their riser spots, gaffer tape with letters in the middle. Tripods are set up and the chairs are out and the national media mills about doing what it does best: waiting. It's not yet two in the afternoon and Lieberman won't take the stage until results are in, maybe eleven tonight, but it has already begun. Stephan Savoia from the Associated Press eyes a spot up front near the stage. I think the same thing. Up front is always best. Stephan has been with the AP forever and it's always good to watch those guys. He's known for telling stories, and, if there's a person to know at the White House, he's got their home number in his Blackberry. He says hi and we discuss the advantages and disadvantages of this space and that. We mark nearby spots with tape and set up computers and connect to the hotel free Wi-Fi. He says he'll have a second shooter in the back come game time. Reuters too, and that makes me uneasy, because I'm solo for Getty, and beating one shooter from each national wire is one thing but trying to beat two shooters from each wire is another.

A Lieberman lackey, a college kid with a pockmarked face, swings by to tell us we can't be in front when it starts because that area is specifically designated for supporters. We point to our marked spots nearby, with our names spelled out in tape, and tell him that's where we'll be, and when the kid leaves Stephan and I agree, when it starts we're going right up front. I ask Stephan where he's staying, figuring he's driving home afterwards. He says, right here, did it online this morning, one twenty, they had bigger rooms but I'm only staying the night.

Like so many other events in so many other places, we stand around a spot on the floor, gear piled at our feet, talking to one another of this and that and anyone else who may wander by and desire a chat, and after so many events, this begins to be everybody. We have only hours upon more hours to kill and we are at where we need to be. Every so often there is an interruption by a Lieberman lackey who reminds us that where we stand is for supporters only and that the press must be off to the side and on the risers in the back. Stephan and I continue to assure the lackey's that this is clearly understood, that we're only passing time here for now until the senator comes out later for the big victory speech, at which point we would move to the side to make way for all the supporters. And when the lackey leaves, Ned from Omaha, in town for the convention and chatting us up about camera gear, asks if we think Lieberman will win? We tell him shit no, the guys toast.

There's the little girl from the supermarket earlier in the day. She runs in and out of the growing crowd, entertaining the loitering media with jokes and precious stories. When she nears I say, I saw you earlier, you were at Shaw's when the senator arrived, right? She performs a half-spin pirouette and curtseys. It was a Stop & Shop, she says, and disappears back into the crowd. Her mother tells us how this little girl has been everywhere on the campaign trail and how she knows the senator personally.

He came to her school because she wrote to him about adoption rights.

Really? Adoption rights? She's interested in that?

She's Romanian. She's very knowledgeable. I'm a lobbyist for children adoption rights there, and, as you know, Romania stopped its current practices and closed itself off to outside adoptions.

I really didn't know any of that, but she was attractive and there was time to pass and she spoke with such passion about the difficulties of adoption and third world bureaucracies and the atrocities perpetrated upon children the world over, all of which I agreed with. And her little girl did seem extra smart. But it also made her annoying. She kept interrupting, and just when I'm trying to make the jump from horrible child labor practices in Eastern Europe to complimenting mom's eyes, from nowhere the little girl appears. Knock knock. She waits for an answer like it's a definite and finally a photographer from New York City says, ok whooze dare?

Joe.

Joe who?

Jon't you want to take the stage now Joe?

Afternoon moves into evening and I eat in the hotel's café while Stephan watches the gear and then he goes to eat and I watch the gear and slowly the stage workers give way to the campaign staffers and the volunteers and supporters and people early for the event. After a walk and a stretch I'm back near the front, near my computer and cameras and the woman with the adopted smart girl. Smart girl is nowhere to be seen but mother says she's out back making witty Pro-Joe signs. She reaches for the credentials around my neck.

Where is this one from?

Boston.

And this one?

Iraq.

She makes an ooohh noise and says that's interesting and wants to ask me more questions when from nowhere once again comes her smart little girl with a new homemade sign. Mother says, oh I'd love to discuss that but not with her around, and I want to ask when but she turns to the New York photographer and begins sorting through the credentials around his neck.

Something tickles my ear and a voice whispers heyyy. Turning, a woman stands so close her nose bumps mine. Her face is red and the reek of gin wafts through her glistening pores. Her mouth hangs half-open. She steps back and sways on her feet, narrowing one eye for better focus. She uses the word fuck as a way to enhance the description of eye color and asks, you staying here, but it comes out sounding, you sane ear? She's got a hold of my credentials, pulling on them so I have to turn my face to keep from smelling her breath and maybe accidentally kissing her. What room you in? I don't think, I say, six two nine.

Want my room number?

I say, sure but could you let go of my credentials? She sways and stares from up close so I have to step back. She takes the Sharpie hanging from my shirt pocket. What's your room number?

I think. I say, two six nine.

She writes two six nine on the palm of her hand and leans in so I have to turn my head again and she trips and recovers and mouths two six nine while backing away into the crowd. When I turn, there's the New York photographer, the single mother, and the smart little girl, all looking at me. The photographer gives a thumbs-up, the single mother smiles, and smart little girl says, guess what I'm going to be when I grow up?

Just before eleven we get word Lieberman will be taking the stage. Polls had him losing to Lamont an hour ago. Stephan and I leave our computers ready for transmit and along with the other photographers who've arrived, move to the stage, taking positions directly in front. At once there is a lackey at our backs.

Hey you guys can't be here. HELLO? This is for supporters only. Supporters only here. I need you all to move to the risers in the back or the positions on the side. He gestures to them like an airline steward does to the plane exits. You need to move NOW.

Not moving, we look to where he points. If waiting is what the national press does best, then this is the thing it does second best.

You ALL have to move, NOW.

He is told, no.

You have to.

No, we don't.

Yes you do. You said you would.

Your guy lost: its over.

There is commotion on the stage and the lackey turns to his Blackberry, looking for help, when Senator Lieberman and his wife walk up the steps from behind the giant American flag and the crowd cheers madly like he didn't just lose. He stands and waves and bows ever so slightly, taking in the applause, and his eyes are damp. His wife steps aside, giving him his due. Thirty seconds into the event and I see Stephan move to his computer, but he's got another shooter on the riser in the back and I need to work another thirty seconds before I can move to mine. Lieberman stands at the podium and motions for the crowd to quiet. His voice breaks when he speaks and when it does I jump up from my computer to climb the ladder and shoot over the heads of the people.

When I hit transmit and the little dog runs I wade back into the crowd shooting and see Stephan working at his computer, standing occasionally to shoot a picture on his own ladder. A hand grabs my ass and squeezes and I can smell her breath and do not have to look. Two-six-nine is whispered into my ear and I slip through the crowd back to my computer. Shoot, edit, transmit, shoot, edit, transmit. And as I hunch over my computer, I hear Senator Lieberman saying, what does this country need right now? He's about to answer his own question when a gravelly voice yells out, PEAS, we need PEEEEEEAAAAAASSSSSSS. I jump up on my ladder preparing for his exit and see a beet-faced lackey squiring from the stage a woman who admonishes him for spilling her G & T. Lieberman clutches the hand of a supporter, fights back tears, thanks everyone for all the years, waves, and disappears behind the American flag.

## Liquid Terror

When I wake up the phone's ringing. Or I wake up because the phone's ringing, one or the other. My dislike of morning calls and a now what and I stumble out of bed searching for the noise. It's Craig Allen on the desk in New York, breathing hard. He's talking about the terrorist plot to blow up airliners coming into the United States from London. Thirty-seconds ago I'd been about to roll over for another hours sleep and now I'm telling Craig of course I heard about that, been monitoring it all morning. As we talk I flip open the lid of my computer to play catch-up. It's all over the web. I tell him I'm heading out now.

Five minutes later and I'm on my way to the airport. Some people might think urinating into a Gatorade bottle and finger brushing your teeth on the morning commute disgusting, but it's surely a time saver. As I drive, I listen to WBZ news and check my hair in the rear view, wetting down a cowlick with spit, and when I pass through the tunnel connector near the spot where Del Valle was killed, I can't help but look up. A reporter updates the days' top story. A bunch of Pakistani's living in Britain had been planning a terrorist attack on airlines using liquids that could be mixed into bombs on board the plane. They'd targeted American, Continental, and Delta. My first thought: didn't Delta and Continental go bankrupt years ago?

Arriving at the airport, I park in Terminal E in the limo lot, where we always park whenever we go to the airport to cover a story. I maneuver my car among the numerous TV trucks well set up with lawn chairs, television monitors, and bags from Dunkin Donuts. I interrupt a man reading the *Boston Herald,* working on a bacon egg and cheese and he lowers the paper and mumbles, guys with guns and dogs.

The story is the liquids. The airlines have banned people from flying with them, so water bottles, nail polish remover, shampoo's, tooth paste, and coffee cups, all that overflowing from garbage bins is the money shot.

Inside I see Cj Gunther from European Pressphoto Agency up on the overhang in Terminal C. Years ago, while still working as a waiter at the Casablanca, I took a freelance assignment to shoot an arraignment at Brookline District court. Some guy killed his girlfriend, lit his house on fire, and jumped out the window. It was a typical starter job in the business--non-paying for a soon-to-be-defunct weekly, that would give me a byline, *if* they used the photo. My first courtroom shoot, and nerves kept me up all night wondering how to do it. I arrived early the next morning to the courthouse and was told I would be the only photographer allowed inside. Moments later another photographer arrived. He's freelancing for the Associated Press and has camera gear and appears to know what he's doing. He wants to be the inside shooter and says he can send me over a photo later on in the day. For some reason I don't agree. He's starting out his career and is under pressure to get inside that courtroom and I'm starting out mine. We face off and eventually the judge allows both of us in. And we've been doing that ever since.

Cj says Phil's around and we should go find him. Phil Orlandella is the spokesman for the Massachusetts Port Authority overseeing the airport. Bad weather, holiday travel backups, he's the guy on television letting everyone know it's business as usual. He's got a way with words.

We find him doing a television interview. The reporter wears lipstick and a crisp red pants suit. When they finish, she thanks him for his time and walks off. We say, hey Phil what's the deal, we need checkpoints. He holds up his finger as if testing wind direction. You can shoot at the checkpoints, just not security itself, the barrels and the garbage, whatever. He seems preoccupied with the red pants suit disappearing into the crowds of pissed-off delayed fliers. He says, you hear the one about Turner Brown? And we say we have not heard the one about Turner Brown, and he tells a joke that ends with, I thought you said turn around.

Back in Terminal E, I'm writing captions and transmitting photos when it dawns on me that eleven days from now I will return to this terminal for the flight to Africa. The thought comes with anxiety. On the Internet is a story. Massachusetts Governor Mitt Romney is preparing to activate the National Guard to secure airports and subways. Boston itself was not a specific target, but he's doing it anyway, precautionary tactics, deputizing fifty members of the 972$^{nd}$ MP's, to be deployed immediately tomorrow. Only one other governor in the country is doing the same: Arrrrnnnold.

National Guard PAO Winfield Danielson answers on the first ring. He says he's sending out a press release within the hour about when exactly the 972$^{nd}$ will be arriving at Logan, he doesn't know for sure yet, but figures it to be sometime around eight in the morning.

The day drains on and there's not too much to shoot but New York wants me to stay with it. It's running strong on all the news sites and they figure it's best for me to return tomorrow for the shots of the Massachusetts National Guard soldiers patrolling and also more pictures of overflowing garbage bins and long lines and mothers throwing away bottles of breast milk. I agree. It's another day rate, and I'm about to hang up when that last one hits me. Breast what? Breast milk. Might not have happened, but if you see it, shoot it.

There's another story breaking, one spawned from the days events. It's being reported that Senator Joe Lieberman has re-gained support from all the people who days before failed to vote for him. With this newest terrorist scare the war has returned to the peoples minds and it's being said that he might have a chance now after all in November, when he could run as an Independent. I flip the computer shut wondering about it all, and head off to security to photograph garbage cans and mothers throwing out breast milk.

. . .

At quarter to seven the next morning, I'm back in the limo lot at Terminal E. Not much reason for arriving so early except all the same reasons for being early. There are the news trucks, still idling their engines, waiting to go live with the day's first update. It's still the top story and I need to get stuff and get it on the wire quick, hygiene not being a good enough excuse for missing the shots of Massachusetts National Guard soldiers jumping from buses with weapons and war paint.

In Terminal C, PAO Danielson is doing a TV interview. The reporter asks a question and as she does, three National Guard soldiers walk past in the background. When they walk out of the camera shot the reporter halts Danielson and has the soldiers back up and do it again. She seems happy with the third take.

Danielson is saying that the role of the National Guard at the airport will be presence, visible but low key, *in the background*. So now I need photos of visible but low-key soldiers in the background. In Terminal E, I buy a coffee at Dunkin' Donuts and juggle the piping hot medium ONE sugar along with my equipment when I see four National Guard soldiers walking across the terminal looking very visible but entirely low key. No time to check camera settings. I shoot pictures walking backward holding the coffee in my left hand and the serious faced soldiers break into giggles just before they disappear behind a door marked Personnel Only. What the hell, it is what it is, but sometimes that leaves an empty feeling. I send three pictures to the desk in New York. Then it's back to Terminal C where Phil has set up a pool shoot.

A pool shoot is where one organization shoots an event and shares it with everyone else. But no one in wire photography likes to share and it can get messy. These days' pool shoots are all too common, and most news organizations fight like hell to be the pool shooter. As a day rater, my theory is just tell me what time I need to show up to get the shared photos, and if they could be emailed, that would be even better.

In the parking lot outside Terminal E, there's Neal Hamberg with Bloomberg. With him is George Rizer. George is with the *Boston Globe.* He tells us he got picked to shoot the pool because he was the first one there at the airport. Unless you got here before me, he asks, I got here at seven, when you get here? Neal says after that and I say way after that.

George has a police scanner pinned to his chest that's squawking like a crazed parrot. It knows where all the fires and shootings are happening. He's half-in and half-out of his car, putting a lens on one camera and a flash on the other. What do you think the exposure will be, and he takes a picture of me and Neal. He looks at the back of his camera like he's confused and never done it before. I gotta set up another camera, I don't know, what do you think? George has been with the *Globe* for somewhere around forty years. He cruises mostly, knows all the streets of Boston and gets to fires and shootings in minutes, sometimes before the bullets stop. He's never missed a picture in his life but right now he's worried about blowing a staged photo-op. Flash no-flash, that look sharp to you? Then again, if it was me, I'd be doing the same thing. We assure him all is fine and head off for the day's nine am news event.

Phil's there and some TV cameras and Elise Amendola with Associated Press sitting on the floor with her laptop plugged into the wall. Elise serves as a reminder, one of my worst failures in the business. My worst. Just a year with Getty, new to the wire industry, and Viviana flies into Boston from Argentina on the same day her country collapses financially. She gets on the plane in Buenos Aires and she's got money in the bank and a working credit card. She gets off and she's got nothing, her family destitute. On the same day a man with religious delusions gets on a flight in Paris with plastic explosives tucked into his sneakers. I'm at the airport waiting for Vivi even as the delusional man's flight is diverted to Boston because he can't light a match. Vivi is late. She's fraught with fear for her family and we watch on television as her fellow countrymen are hit with water canons in front of the Casa Rosada. We attend a Christmas party in Somerville and in the morning when I go to get my papers, there is a headline story from Boston, and a shot on all the covers. It's a picture made through the windshield of a moving car, at night, with flash, a difficult to near impossible photo to make. Elise made it.

Neal and I take seats on the floor and plug in our own laptops and we bid George good luck and he's still talking exposure and flash when he disappears with Phil and the National Guard soldiers pulled for the picture. I check the Getty site to see if my earlier sent photos have been posted and see they have not. I call the desk to ask about it and they say they're moving them now. Irritated I hang up. George returns. It's been less than two minutes.

It was a joke, they did nothing, they just stood there. I didn't know what to do, I took photos of them just standing there, doing nothing.

He tosses camera chips and we ingest them and edit them and chose the same photos and caption and send them. We know it's laughable, this photo of a National Guard soldier poking through a woman's handbag while a photographer snaps a photo, and when the photographer stops snapping the soldiers stop poking, but it is what its become. I send two photos to the desk in New York and follow it with a call. They say they're only moving two pictures from the three I sent earlier because the other one was motion blurred. I tell them fine and I'm going home because this story sucks and if I'm going to shoot shitty photos you should fucking move them. The desk doesn't mind, they're used to ranting photogs. They say have a good day. The breast milk angle never really panned out, and now the story wanes. I'm angry and feel it's all my fault because I didn't get any good stuff, and on the way out I run into Jessica Rinaldi. She's panting and in a rush. She asks, what's happening? I tell her, nothing, it's all bullshit. She says Reuters called when they started seeing stuff on the wire from me and Elise. She's trying to catch her breath, looking around saying she really needs to get a shot of a soldier patrolling. There's pool shit, I tell her, the others have it, they're in Terminal C. She says thanks and runs off. Just as she leaves two National Guardsmen walk towards me and as they pass I raise my camera one-handed and shoot two pictures. When I get home I send them to New York.

That night on television, National Guard PAO Winfield Danielson is interviewed. As he speaks, soldiers walk with exact timeliness into and out of the camera shot and in the morning on the second page of the *Boston Globe* is the photo I took one-handed, illustrating the story of the deployment of the Massachusetts National Guard to Logan Airport in the fight against liquid terror.


*August 17, 2006*
*New Haven, Connecticut, Yale School of Medicine*

Ned Lamont is having a rally with former U.S. Senator John Edwards here in a courtyard. It's his first big event since becoming the U.S. Senate Democratic nominee. At first I thought I took the wrong exit off the highway because it was a bad neighborhood. It turns out that's where Yale is.

Malcolm gets in Saturday so this will be my last assignment before I go. My passport and visa are in and Conway says the paperwork should be ready and waiting when we arrive. Next week this time I'll be in Chad.

My father tells me he goes in to the hospital Tuesday to get checked for the aortic aneurism. Uncle Donny had his surgery, eight hours, and now he's looking at months of rehabilitation. When my father explains this he uses specific words and I know he's back a week from Turkey and bored and researching medical stuff on the Internet. He doesn't say much except if he does have it then I need to get checked because my chances of having it go up. Tuesday, he says, he'll know for sure. Tuesday is the day I leave for Chad.

It's been on my mind, the whole health and safety thing. Not the time for it, but I can't stop thinking about it. Hospitals are like schools to me. I don't like going near them. With no insurance, I'd be going to the downtown hospitals and not the leafy suburban ones. No, my father does not have it so that I don't have it and my daily heartburn is only acid reflux. I just need to stop eating cheese.

A small crowd has gathered and I stand alongside Bob Child near the stage. A young Lamont lackey comes by and tells us we need to stand off to the side or be in the buffer when the event begins because the space up front is designated specifically for supporters. We assure the lackey we plan on moving aside when it all begins and that we are only passing time here for now. Above the heads of the slim crowd a baby girl balances on the shoulders of her father who is the Jew for Lamont from election day. His wife inquires about sun block for the forehead of the baby and she is dismissed with a wave of the hand.

The sun falls and we test the light with shots of the American flag hung for background and hope that it begins soon and not five minutes from now when the light will sink and suck. Six minutes later, Edwards takes the stage and the light cuts him off at the neck, then at his chin, then at his forehead. He's vibrant and it appears he's the man headed to the U.S Senate and not the other man who now stands awkwardly at the back of the stage, lost in the shadows. Edwards steps to the front, catching the last of the light and in it he's golden and he too has a Kennedy look and the people cheer when he begins his introduction of Lamont. He speaks of a recent trip he took to Africa, and when he mentions Sudan, people cheer, and when he mentions Darfur, people cheer, and when he mentions helping refugees, people cheer. I pray he mentions Chad, but he does not.

The stage is dismantled and I transmit my photos to New York, and as the evening falls Child says, goodbye, take care, good luck in-where you going again? I tell him Chad and he says, good luck in Chad. Then I run to my car through the dark and deserted streets of Yale University.

## All The Kennedys Are Dead

Going over the pass, I contemplate crashing my rent-a-car into the snow bank off the side of the road. I don't want to get too hurt, just a little hurt. Dent the car, bump the forehead, deploy the air bags, a trip to the hospital as proof. That should get me out of it.

It's my first travel assignment since going down with a broken foot covering the aftermath of 9/11. I got the call in early January from Mish Coffey on the desk. It was below zero and I was standing outside Middlesex Superior Court in Cambridge, waiting to see if I could get a shot of the Hockey Dad. He's called the Hockey Dad because he beat to death another hockey dad at their sons' hockey practice because of some rough hockey play. Their hockey sons watched it all happen. The Hockey Dads lawyer claimed his client was simply a gentle giant, simply defending himself against an enraged one hundred pound lighter man with a bad temper. He should not go to jail, his lawyer said, because he didn't mean to beat the other man to death, just meant to beat him a little.

When I hear Mish's voice and she asks, so you still want to travel, my heart soars. She knows I want Afghanistan. She's know I've wanted it since 9/11, but breaking my foot kept me from it, and, since then, I'd watched the others leave and return. Was this it? Was it finally my time? Back in the offices, I knew there was talk of moving the Boston position to Los Angeles. The term being used was celebrity photojournalist. Maybe this was just their way of getting their use out of me before giving me the ultimatum, move or quit. I didn't mind, they could shit can me, as long as I got to Afghanistan first.

In late 1999, Gamma Liaison Photo Agency morphed into an online photo agency. It became known as Getty Images. They were hiring regional staffers. I knew people, had affiliations in the office, and drove down to New York City one day. Georges De Keerle held my slide sheets up to the fluorescents lights.

Would you be willing to work with us?

The next week I return to New York to what I thought would be more people meeting and an official interview. In an office with a view of the Trident Building, I told Georges and Richard Ellis of my vision of doing good work, work I cared about, work that mattered, work that helped and forwarded the company. They agreed and nodded. I told them how I thought great things would happen and I truly hoped they'd happen while I worked for them and this growing news agency. They said, absolutely, how much do you want?

It was my first salary negotiation. At the last job I was told straight out, you're making seventeen five. But this was New York City. I looked them in the eye.

I'll take thirty two.

We'll give you forty, and we all stood up and shook hands.

It was like going from the minors to the majors. But I soon learned: in the minors, you play for heart and in the majors, it's all for money. Still, it was a dream job, and I knew it was shooting pictures for the fastest-growing photography news wire in the country, even if sometimes the pictures seemed pointless, like ducks on the Common. The first year I shot signs and storefronts, and sometimes, late at night, I wondered if I'd made the right choice.

But hearing Mish's voice, and she sounds excited for me, I know I'm getting a good one. I take a deep breath and say to her question, yes, totally ready to travel, and in my head I chant, *please say Afghanistan, please say Afghanistan.* I'd never been more depressed than while lying on the couch with my broken foot and watching the news on television, and one morning hobbling down to the corner store for a newspaper and seeing on the cover of every single one pictures by Tyler Hicks, a Taliban fighter being executed outside the gate at Bagram. Three frames. Brilliant. The last I'd seen of Tyler he was sitting in the offices at Getty making plans to go. Then they were talking about his photos on television and radio. I stopped answering my phone and gave up reading newspapers for the next two weeks.

Mish says, so you wanna go to…

*Yes, yes I do.*
…Utah, to cover the Sundance Film Festival?
U-what?
Utah.
*No, no I don't.*
On the first day there I drove from Salt Lake City to Park City to pick up my credentials and get the lay of how it all worked. This was my first major film festival coverage. At media sign-in, the snooty man says, we don't have any Getty on the list. I panic because without credentials, I'd be unable to get into the events. I called the entertainment editor in New York to see why we weren't on the credential list like he had said we were. He doesn't know but promises to make calls, and before I can hang up Georges is on the phone. In the whole office, he is the only guy I don't want to talk to.
Why are you calling here?
We aren't credentialed for the film festival.
So what? I don't want to hear this. This is your first trip for us. I want to hear you'll get it done. That's what I want to hear.
I didn't remind him it wasn't my first travel assignment, as I did go to New York following the Trade Center attacks and also that seal hunt in the Gulf of Saint Lawrence and that sex-toy story in Toronto. But it was Georges who was the instigator behind getting the Boston position moved to L.A. His idea of good photojournalism was any picture that made money, and usually that involved a celebrity. He understood the business was in flux and he had Sargent's ear, the main man with hiring and firing, and I'd had a bad feeling ever since he gave his "photojournalism is dead speech" to me and Raedle at the post 9/11 dinner at Half King. We laughed along with him at his prediction, because Georges is a man hard not to like, though you may try, and tried to ignore the pieces of truth.

You don't need credentials, Georges said, you just need to go into the hotels and find them. Get them coming from their rooms, in the lobby, go up and take their pictures. Do you understand?

I did. It was on the drive back to Salt Lake when the thoughts of crashing my rent-a-car into a snow bank began.

By week's end, I am a seasoned entertainment photojournalist. I yell JEN BRAD, over here right here look at me thank you oh that's nice thank you that's nice you're hot so hot thanks Brad, JEN over here, with the best of them. On Main Street, outside the movie theater, is Mariah Carey, and I rush to her and blast her point-blank, slamming flash into her face before she's recognized and makes a getaway in a black SUV. I stop Andy Garcia and say, smile. We get credentialed after all, and there are multiple premieres a night, between three, four, and five venues. I make friends with the other celebrity photographers and we travel in packs around Park City deciding which premiere is most important because of who's in the movie and who will be there. Each night after the last premiere, I drive back over the pass to my room in Salt Lake and work on photos and transmit until four in the morning. Then it's a little sleep and back to the pack and Park City for another day of screaming. ROBIN-OVER HERE, oh you're funny, that's funny, whose hat is it Robin? It's your hat. Right here Robin, right here, thank you, thank you.

The last premiere of the festival is a Russell Crowe indie movie. It's slated for midnight. I'd been at it two weeks and was running tired, looking forward to the flight home. We arrived for the screening early and stood behind the velvet rope. It's so cold I take the batteries out of my cameras and warm them in my jacket underneath my armpits. Crowe's late. It's well past one in the morning when he arrives and walks quickly past the waiting press. My batteries are dulled, my senses sluggish, my auto-focus creaks and I shoot blurry pictures. All I needed was a picture of Crowe walking past and I could have felt good about my coverage, and I miss it. I check with the others and some had better angles and some did okay, but everyone agrees, Russell Crowe is an asshole.

In the morning I'll be hearing from Georges about the missing Crowe pictures. He would be right, fuck it, miss is miss. I just didn't need to hear it from him.

Next morning I'm watching it snow outside the airport windows. The flakes are light and I tap my foot waiting, slumped in my seat, too tired to read, exhaustion hitting after the weeks of work and last night until five in the morning. We board the plane, well late, and I'd already missed the Phoenix connection and now wouldn't be home until after midnight. Waiting for taxi to the runway the phone rings. I don't even have to look.

Nice job, Georges says. You did well. Nice shot of Mariah on Main Street, only you gave her short legs.

Short what?

Legs. You shot her vertical with a wide. You need to get the middle lens like the others, so they don't have short legs.

Looking out the window, the snow falls harder, and though we don't move, the stewardess stops and tells me to hang up the phone.

Georges, we're about to take off. I have to go. *And I've heard this before. Re-structuring…lost the edge…*

Think about LA. Seriously. Look at the big picture. Everybody wants to be a photojournalist but there is only one James Nachtwey. There is no more news in the northeast. All the Kennedys are dead.

Sargent called me the last day of February to say the Boston position was being dissolved. It was LA by April first. I asked for a few days to think it over but I knew before I hung up the phone. The following month I become a freelancer, again, working for the same company that had just laid me off, wondering if it was over before it even started.

## Last Minute Nothing

There are so many things to do but they are little things and I've never been good with those. I have learned that when you have little things to do, it is best to wake early and begin promptly. So I'm up at nine thirty and for the next hour and a half I read the morning papers and when the phone rings I don't look to see who it is. Whatever they may have to say I most likely do not want to hear. Can you shoot Monday? Where? Can you recommend someone else? Thanks, good luck in...where did you say you're going again?

First on the list of little things is a thing-a-ma jig to recharge camera batteries from a car battery. It's a just-in-case. Over the years I've purchased all the just-in-case power sources available in the first world. They take up bag space and have been carted to third worlds, going unused and left behind. But the just-in-case realities of digital photography are real, no electricity means no pictures, and Lydia Polgreen, *The New York Times* Africa correspondent, confirmed that power is a major issue in Chad.

To the salesman at Radio Shack I describe what I need by holding up my hands and telling him it should be able to charge computers and camera batteries off a car battery.

He says he's got just the thing, a 359-Watt DC to AC Power Inverter, runs off the battery of a car with little jumper cables or right from the cigarette lighter. It equips the vehicle with two power outlets.

What if I don't have a car?

Then you need this, and he's pointing to a suitcase looking thing-a-ma-jig, describing how that baby can light a small village, when I cut him off and pay the sixty-four and change.

Heading to Calumet Photo, I cross the river on the BU Bridge and the years run through my mind. It was just up the way that I stood on the corner that summer day I quit the security of the Casablanca for a life of photojournalism, wondering how and if I would ever make a living in the business. There, where I made the pictures of the Ivy League rowing teams practicing for the Regatta against a red sun, and over there, where I set up my tripod for the Fourth of July fireworks celebration. Storm pictures of Boston's skyline are always good from along the river's edge, and once I kissed a girl there too, my first kiss after landing in Boston, after being kicked from the U.K. She threw up later, but anyway I kissed her. I need a four gigabyte memory card, don't forget, and call Matt before you leave, make sure. This bridge is old and shitty. I can't believe it hasn't fallen in yet. They should have built the Big Dig this shitty. Where the white geese congregate is where I hung with the homeless guys who told me to fuck off but then invited me into their camp. I owe Glen two hundred for this months rent on the studio plus two hundred from last month. Remember, don't call Glen before you leave.

I buy memory cards for my cameras and two more digital batteries and twelve rolls of color film. The salesman gives me an odd look when I ask for the film and I explain it's just in case there's no electricity and my thing-a-ma jig doesn't work or I don't have a car.

For some reason this leaves me exhausted and when I get home I sort through the mail on the porch step that piles up because my roommate, Joanna, never picks hers up and I only do sometimes. There's an envelope from a Dr. Steven Keenholtz who owns the clinic where I got the yellow fever shots. It's the second time I've gone to the clinic and I've yet to meet Dr. Keenholtz. I've met three other people and the person I deal with is Nurse Kathleen. Nurse Kathleen likes to have talks with me, discussions about disease and health and the common sense one should have when it comes to these things. She always appears genuinely concerned for my well being. When I went to Iraq last minute, Nurse Kathleen explained to me all the diseases I could possibly get there. She would say, you really should have this shot, and I would say, how much does that shot cost?

The last time I went she gave me a hepatitis shot and told me to return for a follow-up shot when I got back from overseas. I promised her I would and never returned. But the yellow fever shots are mandatory for entering Chad so when I arrive at the clinic in Danvers, Nurse Kathleen is waiting for me with the big hep needle and her book of infectious diseases. She knows I have a fear of needles because I confessed this the first time I went. Nurse Kathleen has the demeanor of a long time medical professional and when I confessed how deep my fear of needles was she said, oohh, what a baby, and slammed one into my shoulder. She asked if it hurt and when I said a little she slammed in another one and asked, how about that one?

Nurse Kathleen scolds me for not returning for the follow up hepatitis shot and explains there are many possible diseases I could get in Chad. She's got her book open and recommends half a dozen shots but eventually admits that most of the shots only prevent nonfatal diseases. She's sticking away and I face the wall while she asks if I need more malaria pills. Malaria is prevalent in Chad, she says. I tell her about the pants I bought at EMS with mosquito repellent built right in. She continues sticking up to three hundred dollars worth, and I put it on my credit card, for the miles. That was two weeks ago and the bill in my hand says this Keenholtz guy wants another one hundred fifteen dollars. I search for exactly why on the bill, an explanation, but there is none, just a breakdown of the shots and a "please pay this amount." I call the number on the bill and a woman answers. I launch into why I'm calling, about having paid three hundred and twenty dollars for four shots two weeks ago that made me sick to my stomach, even though Nurse Kathleen said they wouldn't, when the woman interrupts me.

May I take your number?

Take my number? Can't I just tell you my problem and you patch me through to Keenholtz or look it up on the computer?

This is a message service. What number can you be reached at?

This isn't the office?

No, it's a message service. Can I take your number and have him call you Monday morning.

Let me ask you lady, you ever met this Keenholtz?

•  •  •

Malcolm's plane is due in today at twelve-thirty six. At twelve forty I roll into the airport and park at the curb. I don't want to pay for parking so I call him on his cell phone. I get his voice mail and tell him to walk outside the doors and keep walking until he sees me. A state trooper waves at my car, so I do the loop around and park back in the same spot moments later. We play this game twice more. Malcolm calls and says he's walking out now and I see him through the rear view. With his white beard and worn knapsack he looks like a homeless guy. He throws his bags into the back seat. I haven't seen Malcolm in over two years.

Hey.

Hey.

Hows things?

Good.

How was the flight?

Good.

Good.

On the front porch with the sun setting, we finish off a twelve pack and smoke a joint, discussing dinner plans. He's listening to me describe Gary's restaurant, Oleana, and how it's a dining experience and how I know Chef Ana personally, who always sends out free appies. He agrees it would be nice to eat a good meal, one last one before we head off to eat who knows what for the next three weeks. While he cracks another beer, I tell him about the Mediterranean spices that make Ana's food unique and of the James Beard Award she won recently. He says wow, and we light another joint, watch the sun drop, and call for takeout pizza.


## The Pack

The equipment I take is spread across the middle room of the apartment. I don't know if this irritates Joanna, but, among things that do: motorists who don't use turns signals, people who miscategorize recyclables, and those who overwater plants to the point where the water flows down the bookshelf onto *her* books. Knowing I will be gone near a month, she says nothing as I spread out the gear and my travel bags and begin looking it over for the perfect configuration. Since Malcolm arrived we'd been running all the little errands I'd been putting off and the reality of the trip has begun to wash over me. I sit on the floor and put things into place, a lens here, camera body there, vitamin C packets stuffed between to snug it up. My phone rings. For some time now I have been dodging the woman I'd been dating. I'd been dodging a good many people but of them all, her in particular. She would call and leave a message and I would wait until the next day when she was at work and call her at home. Finally I know it's time to deal. I crack a Sam Adams and walk onto the porch.

Like I saw her that morning I say, hi, how are you? I know, so busy. What am I up to? Packing, it's all over the apartment. What, right around the corner? Sure, swing by.

Looking up the road I see her car turning onto the street. I've got minutes to shake the cool afternoon buzz. I need to concentrate and push away the daydreams. Malcolm reads in the rocker by the windows. He looks serenely happy in the light and I want to be him.

For the next two hours I sit and listen as she tells of the time she backpacked Africa. I place things in my bag and take them out and tell her keep talking. I try to do what I need to do but I'm having trouble. It had never been that I didn't want to see her, more that I wanted to forget her for a while: her voice, and the ways she had, blowing the hair from her face or how her eyes crinkled up when she laughed. She was soft and sweet and where I was going there was none of that. The forgetting of here softened the landing of there. I needed time and distance between those two things but now she sits on the living room floor cross-legged and tells of the time she caught the bus out of Bangui. Now I am not thinking of Chad or Africa or the journey. My head is clouded and I resent Malcolm and wish he would go. She stands and arches her lithe body, saying keep in touch, send emails. My fingertips touch her silky sundress.

Into the twenty two by fourteen by nine inch Tamron backpack I stuff a Canon G11 video camera, a Nikon D1X, a Nikon D1H, an FM2, one Nikon 17-35 2.8 lens, one Nikon 50mm 1.2 lens, one Nikon AF-VR Nikkor 80-400 4.5/5.6D lens, one SB-80DX flash, 6 ULTRA HIGH POWER nickel metal-hydride 7.2v rechargeable batteries, two Nikon MH-16 chargers, an assortment of odds and ends, and my new thing-a-ma-jig that charges off a car battery or cigarette lighter. This will be my carry on, along with my computer bag that holds the Dell Latitude C400, a dozen CD/DVD's, backup hard drives, notebooks, pens, Ethernet cables and converters. My check in bag has two pair of EMS cargo pants, three shirts, eight pairs of socks, four pairs of underwear, two-dozen Power Bars, beef jerky, and a forty-two pack of Prilosec OTC.

Malcolm is finished reading. He wants to go to Oleana for dinner. He says the Mediterranean spices sound good. The scent of her lingers in the room. I can still hear her voice. I tell Malcolm pizza is fine by me and go for a jog around the pond.

## Departure

We arrive at the airport five hours early. Malcolm isn't happy with leaving the house at two o'clock for an eight o'clock flight but I'm anxious and keep looking at the watch I now wear. It's half the reason I never wear watches. In between I fussed with my bag, lifting it and setting it down, feeling it get heavier with each hoist. Finally Malcolm says, let's go. We say goodbye to Joanna who spins in her chair and bids us a good and safe trip. The walk to the T station takes tens minutes and along the way I point out the house I stayed in after the time I got thrown from the UK for looking like a migrant laborer. Malcolm walks quickly and ahead and I explain to his back that leaving early is good because anything can happen like long transfers and we have three of those. The first train to Downtown Crossing arrives moments after we enter the station. I smile at Malcolm. Never happens, generally its forever. He picks up a newspaper from the floor. The ride into the city seems faster than usual and when we step from one train to the other now bound for the airport I say, this is unbelievable. At the end of the line, the shuttlebus waits, and five minutes after that we walk into Terminal E at Logan International, and as I'm saying, I've never done it that fast, Malcolm turns and walks away.

Standing in line, an Air France worker tags the bags, working his way person-by-person closer. When he tags a bag that appears similar in size and weight to mine, I am elated. But when he points to another bag similar to mine and does not tag it, I rehearse the arguments I have prepared for the very moment. He nears and I hold out my computer bag, sliding my camera bag along the floor attempting to make it look light. He tags the computer bag and runs his eyes over the other bag. You gotta check it. I hear me say, no way it's camera gear, I measured it, it conforms to regulations-I've been on your web site, until he bends over the bag and lifts it six inches off the ground, gauges the weight, and drops it with a thud. He shrugs, deal with it at the counter.

Every fucking time.

Malcolm tells me to relax, which is easy for him, because he's carrying notebooks. Years ago on a trip to Argentina in this airport in this terminal, the airline I was flying deemed this very bag to be too big. A manager was hailed and I was told firmly either check the bag or don't fly. I stood at the counter and strapped both high-end digital cameras over my shoulders and stuffed the thousands of dollars in lenses into my pockets. Fellow flyers commented on the gear as I took my seat. Argentina had just suffered an economic crash and the politicians and foreign bankers had flown all the money out of the country and there was still a corralito in effect. Viviana said to be as inconspicuous as possible, you don't want to be sequestro expresso, she had half joked. When I stepped off the plane in Mendoza she suggested I go somewhere and put the shiny expensive camera gear out of sight before we exited the airport into the throngs of desperate men offering taxi rides for a dollar and phone cards for pennies.

Standing in line I vacillate between nervous and angry for the next fifteen minutes while people in front of me check in with small to gargantuan bags. When it comes my turn, I take a deep breath and slide my bag along the floor with my foot, to the counter. I fumble with my passport, looking confused. No one likes to deal with an idiot.

Hi, how are you today? I smile. The ticket man says nothing and takes my passport and thumbs through it. I hold the smile. Malcolm is already getting his tickets punched. With his thick beard and camouflage clothing he looks just this side of a terrorist. His ticket agent says, thank you for flying Air France. My ticket agent ignores my smile and continues to look through my passport. He keeps going past the page with my picture and thumbing back through, landing on the page with the Venezuelan visa.

Do you have a green card?

He's beating me at my own game. I let the question hang, and in my head say, come on buddy I got Beantown Irish stamped all over me, look at my forehead, its peeling from the twenty minutes of sun I got earlier today, racial profile me. Out loud I say, green cahd, you kiddin'?

He flips through the pages looking at the visas and back up at me. Finally he finds my picture on the inside cover flap...where they always put it.

Do you have a visa for, he scrutinizes the ticket, for where you're going?

Chad, I say, yes I do have a visa, and in what I am sure is a breach of Homeland Security, reach across the counter and point to the visa, issued on the last page before there are no more stamps.

Oh, because of the T.

That's how they spell Tchad in Chad.

The printer spits out tickets. The agent inquires about baggage and I place the check-in onto the scale. It weighs close to nothing. The man working the scale launches my bag onto the conveyor belt. He points, what about that one?

That's just carry on.

What's that?

Computer.

He's suspicious, looking at me as if I've broken well-known travel baggage laws. Walking over, he lifts my camera bag and throws it onto the scale like it's definitely not camera gear. I'm sweating and fidgeting and want to kill this baggage man. Malcolm has inched closer to watch. The scale leaps and falls and settles.

Too much, check it.

The guy has a flashlight and a nametag but he seems to be the boss when it comes to bag-weight issues, and another man reaches for the bag to put it on the conveyor. I go now into Act Two.

Wo, wait, no way Chief, I'm not checking that. This is camera gear and I'm a photographer going on a business trip and there's no way it's going under the plane.

I do it for effect, with a Boston accent, because it's worked before. I pull the zipper down the sides of the bag and lay it open to reveal the tens of thousands of dollars worth of gear. It gleams under the lights. Crowds gather and admire and a conversation begins among airport personnel, Nikon V Canon, and one man whistles through his teeth, supe caro.

It's still not looking good and I think about going into Act Three, where I pull up my shirt and begin pointing to fat people. But the man with the flashlight says, just give him some, and he points to Malcolm. I give Malcolm my 80-400 and the bag is re-weighed and the scale leaps and falls and settles and the ticket agent hands me my ticket.

As we walk to security, Malcolm hands me back my lens and I stuff it into my carry on. With his small bag he sales through security but my necklaces and bracelets make the scanners beep and so I have to walk back through and take off the jewelry and shoes. When I go through again the security man says, stand there, pointing to two footprints painted onto the carpet. He gives me a rub down and I feel his breath in my ear.

What's this?

Money pouch, I whisper.

How much, he says loudly.

Two thousand eight hundred and fifty-six, I say, pulling out the pouch. I don't want Malcolm to hear because we said we'd bring the same amount of money and he said he was bringing thirty five hundred.

You don't carry traveler's checks?

*Does anyone carry traveler's check?* They don't work well where I'm going.

Where you going?

Chad?

Where?

Near Darfur.

He hands me back the money pouch. You going there? Man, let me know if you need any security, he says, as if I'd hire him on the spot and he would quit his job and get on the plane with me. Security. So far I had been at the airport for twenty minutes and already my fellow travelers knew where I was going, what I did for work, that I carried a lot of expensive camera gear with me, and had a money pouch stuffed full of cash down the back of my pants.

I'll let you know.

We go to the bar and sit and order beers and take out books and commence with the three weeks of ignoring each other. My cell phone rings and I know who it is because I've been waiting for the call

Son?

Ya.

All is fine.

Nothing?

Nothing.

He tells me to have a good trip. I think; I just might.

THE END

Made in the USA
Charleston, SC
25 November 2012